CHINA:

The Revolution Continued

CHINA:

The Revolution Continued

JAN MYRDAL and GUN KESSLE

Translated from the
Revised Swedish Edition by
Paul Britten Austin

VINTAGE BOOKS
A Division of Random House/New York

To the memory of
Li Yiu-hua, "The Old Secretary"

died of stomach cancer

August 1965

Explanation of Terms Used

1 yuan, Y	Roughly 42 U.S. cents
1 chi	13¼ inches
1 li	550 yards
1 jin	1 lb. 1½ oz.
1 mu	.9 rood
kang	The domestic clay bed that is heated from underneath
"Sixteen Points"	The Central Committee's resolution of August 8, 1966, which drew up the main directives of the cultural revolution
silver dollar	Corresponds in principle to the silver value of the Mexican dollar
loess	Layers of wind-blown soil. Fertile. Forms huge deposits in which the rain cuts deep ravines
1 hectare	2741 acres
yamen	A mandarin's official residence, his offices
hsien	Administrative unit, often translated as "county"
kaoliang	*Sorghum vulgare*, an annual of the grass family *gramineae* grown chiefly in eastern Asia as grain for human and animal use

Contents

Introduction

> To win countrywide victory is only the first step in a long
> march of ten thousand li. Even if this step is worthy of
> pride, it is comparatively tiny; what will be more worthy
> of pride is yet to come. After several decades, the victory
> of the Chinese people's democratic revolution, viewed in
> retrospect, will seem like only a brief prologue to a long
> drama. A drama begins with a prologue, but the prologue
> is not the climax. The Chinese revolution is great, but
> the road after the revolution will be longer, the work
> greater and more arduous.
> —— Mao Tse-tung, Report to the Second Plenary
>   Session of the Seventh Central Committee of
>   the Communist Party of China, March 5, 1949

This is a book about a village in the hinterland of China;
it is a book about the Cultural Revolution. The cultural
revolution is a revolution of great historical importance
for the world; the village is so small it cannot be found
on any map. To view the cultural revolution from "outside," from "above," gives a distorted perspective. Any
reader can go to his local paper and ask for the files from
1966 to 1969 and read what was printed about the cultural
revolution in China. That which was printed by our large
and small newspapers in the United States or Sweden was
very sensational; but as journalism it was more fiction
than fact. If the reports had been correct, then China
would have vanished from the face of the earth.

The reports were not true. They were tailored to fit the
political needs of the hour. They were spread by the misinformation agencies in Hong Kong and Moscow, in
Taipeh and Washington. I say this, but I do not want my
readers just to take my word for it. Here in Sweden the
students have been taking out the files from the big news-

papers, have read them through and reported on what they found. I hope this is being done also in the United States. One does not have to be "left-wing" to do this. Anyone who is able to read can do it. He can draw his own conclusions.

It is good, though, to compare the statements attributed to different Chinese leaders with the official Chinese translations. I can take a Soviet example. January 11, 1969, Pravda carried a long article by O. Lvov: "Political Manoeuvres of the Mao Tse-tung Group." The article begins:

> Events of the past few years show that the Mao group, in its great-power adventurist policy, based on petty-bourgeois nationalist ideology hostile to Marxism-Leninism and proletarian internationalism, is under-mining the positions of socialism in China. The group has realized that, with the usual methods, it will not be able to turn the Chinese working people into "silent cogs" and "obedient sheep" and achieve the aims of its anti-popular, anti-socialist course.
>
> —Quoted from the official Soviet translation to English as published in "Unity" No. 5, 1969, by Novosty Press Agency in Moscow.

The article was written after the Enlarged Twelfth Plenary Session of the Eighth Central Committee of the Chinese Communist Party. As the author O. Lvov puts the expressions "silent cogs" and "obedient sheep" inside quotation marks the reader gains the impression that this expresses the aims of the "Mao group."

But as a matter of fact it does not. If the reader turns to the official press of the period in which this Pravda article was written (the press that this O. Lvov was reading while writing his article) he will find that the shoe is on the other foot. (See for instance *Peking Review* No. 51, 1968, p. 11: "Discrediting the Theory of 'docile tools.'")

It was the "Mao group" who fought against the ideas that people should be "docile tools" or be "obedient."

The misinformation about China has reached such proportions that a conscious effort is needed by the reader who wants to have a clear picture. Take simple things. If I say that liquor is cheaper in the village shop now than in 1962, people will ask: What, are they allowed to take a drink in China? Of course they are. Why should they not be? At festive occasions people drink. Older men take a drink every night during winter. There is very little drunkenness—but that is another question. If I say that I listened to the radio in the village people will ask: What, were you allowed to listen to the radio? What did people say? But the villagers could not care less. They had radios of their own. Transistors are being spread all over China. There is not a village without a radio. In 1962 there was a central radio for the village; in 1969 the families had their own radios.

In the parks of Peking, or on the new bridge at Nanking people will be strolling about on Sunday afternoon. They will be walking with their transistor radios and they will be taking photos of each other. Film is available everywhere. There are many more cameras and many more transistors than in 1962. I have never heard any Chinese say that there is anything counter-revolutionary in people taking photos of each other. Foreigners cannot take what photos they like of the new Nanking bridge. That is natural. Foreigners are not allowed to take photographs in the Stockholm archipelago either. But the Chinese go around taking photos of the new Nanking bridge and the Swedes go around taking photos of the beautiful Stockholm archipelago. It is humiliating to have to write this. Not humiliating to me, but humiliating to the information media who have managed to misinform the public to such a degree that even the simplest facts of everyday life in China (transistors or cameras) sound strange and unbelievable.

The misinformation about China is political. But it does not only help the decision-makers in Moscow, Taipeh, Tokyo, and Washington to keep their own people uninformed. It also means that these decision-makers themselves become uninformed. Intelligence activities—and large sums are being spent on gathering intelligence from China—are no substitute for information. In fact, a situation when the information level is kept low, the intelligence activity high, and the commentators (in this case the "China-watchers" in Hong Kong) fall for every rumor, is very dangerous; will lead to grave mistakes in policy. It is so doing in the United States. I will take an example from recent history, it is an example, not an analogy: In 1933 all the official mass media of Europe were telling of the failure of the five-year plan in the USSR. The Soviet government was toppling. That was the level of public information. The British government spent rather large sums on gathering intelligence from the USSR. Much of this intelligence was valueless (stemming from the *émigré* circles in Tallinn); much was correct insofar as it corresponded to facts, but by being selected from the general viewpoint that the USSR was collapsing, it gave a false general picture. The British ambassador in Moscow at the time, Sir Esmond Ovey, was influenced by this general evaluation and reported accordingly. (Diplomatic reports, as I know those I have read from the Swedish Foreign Service, tend to be no more and no less reliable than the reports published in the official press.)

When the Metropolitan-Vickers case opened in Moscow the British government acted according to the information, intelligence, and diplomatic reports they had available. An embargo was put on Soviet goods. The Soviet government answered with a counter-embargo.

The trade war continued for several months. British economic interests were injured. At last the compromise was reached that the Soviet side had suggested from the beginning. The embargo and counter-embargo were both lifted and the persons condemned to jail at the trial were expelled from the USSR. Through a false assessment of the strength of the USSR, the British government had been led to measures that injured British interests. In the end they gained nothing but lost quite a lot of trade to France in the middle of an economic crisis.

I took this example because it does not concern the outbreak of a war, but of a minor conflict; also because the question at that moment was not whether the members of the British government should "like" or "dislike" the Soviet government (the members of that British government were the most decided foes of the USSR) but that they were not able to take measures apt to the situation, as they were misinformed about the situation.

The reader might say that I am biased in favor of China and the cultural revolution. Of course I am. Nobody can read what I have written these last years without seeing this; the rational and, in my opinion, necessarily determining reasons for this are contained in what I have written. And of course I have changed; the act of writing changes the writer. When I arrived back in the village in 1969 after seven years of absence I did not yet know what I knew when I left. As I have changed through the changing events between 1962 and 1969 so I changed through my experience in the village in 1969.

From a general Chinese point of view, Liu Ling is not average in economic development. It is situated in a poor and economically backward area of China. In agricultural production and in economic development it cannot be compared to the "ordinary Chinese farming villages" of the plains. It is far less developed.

In the Yenan area Liu Ling is not among the economically least successful and not among the economically most successful production brigades; it is not average, it is slightly above average.

The important point here in question is that the under-estimation and the underrating of Chinese agricultural production and rural economic development makes China an enigma. This in turn leads to false conclusions. China has repaid all post-1949 debts, China has a rapidly developing industry, in science and technology China is achieving and surpassing world levels. This would be enigmatic if China had stayed on an Indian level. But once the plain and simple fact of Chinese economic development in the countryside is accepted—that the Chinese are not lying—then the enigma disappears. But if one reads of this village Liu Ling as being "slightly above average" in Chinese rural economic development in general, then the Chinese satellite becomes enigmatic; if one believes that Liu Ling is far above the general economic development in the Chinese countryside; then nothing can be understood any longer.

There is also another dimension to the question of the "typical" and the "average." In the introduction to *Report from a Chinese Village* I used these words in a sense which I later found were not readily understood by many readers. They were not familiar with the distinction between typical and average. Liu Ling is typical, though it is below the general economic average and slightly above the local economic average.

As to the question of choice and choices it is all very simple. You ask to go to a place, you might or might not get permission. This was the same in both 1962–63 and 1969. When you are there you discuss what you want to see and do. If there is any specific place you want to visit you ask for it. Take Liu Ling as an example. A group of my colleagues, journalists, went from Peking on a journey that took them to Yenan in the spring of 1963. I had talked very much about Liu Ling while writing my book in Peking. They asked to go there. The Chinese did not suggest it; the "colleagues" chose to ask for it.

Much has changed during these seven years. This book is a sequel to *Report from a Chinese Village*. I hope that as large a number as possible of my readers will read both books. Only by doing that can they really get a good picture of the change in Liu Ling village. Liu Ling village has changed very much. I describe the change in this book; but it will most clearly be seen by comparing what the people say about themselves in this book with what they told me seven years earlier.

Coming back to Liu Ling was fascinating. I knew it would be. I had asked to go to Liu Ling the moment the Chinese Embassy in Stockholm told me that our old visa applications from 1966 had been approved and that visas were going to be issued. I and Gun Kessle took the matter up as soon as we had arrived in Peking. A week later we were told that the local people in Liu Ling approved of our coming back to visit them.

("The masses have discussed the matter in Liu Ling and said that you are welcome.")

We stayed for a fortnight in Liu Ling. I talked with people; Gun went around taking photographs. She was not accompanied by anyone. She could go wherever she pleased in the neighborhood. She knew the people. She asked for permission before she took photos. She did not go into people's homes before she was invited. But that is normal politeness in Sweden as in China as everywhere. People often complain about difficulties in taking photographs in China. I don't understand them. If anybody barges into my house and starts taking pictures without being invited I kick him out. Whether he is a Swede or a Chinese or an Italian. It has happened that I have had to kick people out of my home because they lack this politeness. (Swedes.) And I do not accept being photographed by press photographers while I am swimming at some beach. Even if it sounds strange to many readers, the Chinese are no more and no less keen on their privacy. I know of people who have had their visas cancelled in China because they have not understood this; but I also know of foreigners who have been beaten up in Sweden for the same reason.

The people in Liu Ling had not received my former book. They knew it had been written. I told them that I had sent it to them in care of the Association in Peking. The people in Liu Ling criticized the officials in Peking for not having done their duty and sent the book to Liu Ling. (This book though—in Swedish—has been sent to Liu Ling and has been received.)

On the fourth night of our new stay in the village Mau Pei-hsin asked me to come to the cave of the doctor, Wang You-nan. Gun had been sitting there for some hours with *Report from a Chinese Village* and most of the young people in the village had gathered there. We went through the book chapter by chapter. They were very interested. I asked what they thought about it. They said that in the main it was correct. I asked what that meant and if they had any specific criticism. They said that as far as they could understand it was correct, but that if they were to make an absolute statement or make specific criticism the whole book would have to be translated into Chinese word by word and they would have to read it carefully and discuss it thoroughly; but as far as they had gathered it was in the main correct.

I am a writer; I am not an intelligence agent. When I—once only—was told that I had asked questions that they were not going to answer—questions about arms and militia—I accepted this. The reason is very simple. I live in the Swedish countryside. I travel much in Sweden. Also in the forests. As is well known the Swedish granite is as full of fortifications as a Swiss cheese is full of holes. I stumble over fortifications and air-strips all over the countryside. I might have my doubts about the efficacy of these defense measures. But I have never dreamed of telling a foreigner where they are or where he can find them. In Liu Ling they did not doubt the efficacy of their defense arrangements; that they did not want to discuss the details with a foreigner was not only understandable. It was as far as I understand most correct.

In this book I have in some chapters given quotes and political explanations. I found them necessary. But I have not been changing (of course) what people told me. Thus when Chi Mei-ying says that formerly 60 per cent of the infants died, that is Chi Mei-ying talking. I take her expression to mean that "in the old society" and before the hygienic campaign and the scientific methods of child-bearing the infant mortality was very, very high. This, I hope, is self-evident.

When we were in Peking a newly arrived Soviet diplomat was going around telling "Westerners" that he had formerly been stationed in Washington. He had been a "China-expert" at the Soviet Embassy in Washington, and he had had the best of contacts with his "counterparts" at the State Department and in the Pentagon. They used to meet regularly to exchange information about China and views of the developments in China. I do not doubt his words. But the information they are exchanging is of little value. A much greater Soviet personality than this diplomat has expressed it very well. I can take his words as a motto for this book:

. . . In order to *observe,* it is necessary to observe far down where one can get a *survey* of how the new life is being built up, in a workers' district in the province or in the countryside . . . not in the center of the furious attacks on the capital, the furious struggle against conspiracies, the frothing fury of the intellectuals of the capital but in the countryside or in a factory in the provinces (or at the front). There it is easy through simple observation to distinguish the decomposing old from the sprouting new. . . .

—V. I. Lenin to A. M. Gorki, July 31, 1919

CHINA:

The Revolution Continued

Liu Ling —Seven Years Afterward

We return to Liu Ling early one morning in late autumn, 1969. The night frost is still lying in the shade. The air is fresh. The village has changed.

The village looks different. In 1962 only the village school and the row of administration offices where we lived were stone caves. The rest were earth caves. The word "cave" is misleading. It takes at least as much labor to build an earthen cave as to build a house. But the earthen cave is the better dwelling. And the stone cave is an unusually stable and well-insulated stone house.

Now the school is to be rebuilt. Stone is being cut for the school caves. In the cave where I used to work in 1962 some students from Sian are now living, and our sleeping cave has been turned into a storehouse. A wing of ten new caves has been built for the needs of the brigade. The doctor's surgery unit, two rooms for meetings (connected by double doors), offices for the labor groups and the brigade (its offices are also used as dwellings).

In the main village, almost half of all households (16 out of 37) have moved into new stone caves. (For the brigade as a whole, 59 out of 161 households have moved into new stone caves). All these have been built during the cultural revolution. They are being built by the brigade's building group. By rationalizing, building costs have been brought down by about 10 per cent during the last three years.

It was in 1966 that the brigade began building stone caves. The idea had been discussed earlier. But it had

3

proved impossible to reach an agreement about the necessary investments. But in 1966, stone caves had been built for the noodle factory.

"During the time this was being built," says Feng Chang-yeh, the question began to be discussed more seriously. It should be possible to realize the idea of rebuilding the entire village. Some thought it impossible. It would cost too much. We discussed the matter many times. We studied Mao Tse-tung. We must learn from the Tachai Brigade in the Shansi Province. We must be capable of changing things ourselves and breaking with poverty and backwardness. Our discussions went on a long time. In the end agreement was reached. That we hadn't realized plans we had had as early as 1962 for rebuilding the village in 1963, 1964, or 1965 was really due to two things. For one, we had not saved enough. If one is to build stone caves, savings are necessary. For another, our policy was wrong. We were following Liu Shao-ch'i's line; and the cadres were not leading the masses along the right path."

The average building cost was 220 Y per cave. People usually built two caves for each family and kept their old earthen cave as a storehouse. In some cases the old earthen cave was used as a dwelling for the older members of the family. Mau Pei-hsin built two stone caves for his family. His father Mau Ke-yeh stayed in the old home.

"The new dwellings," said Mau Pei-hsin, "are better and more roomy. That has many advantages. When one no longer lives in crowded conditions, it's also easier to plan one's family. Those who live too crowded together often find it hard to use contraceptives."

Building costs could vary according to where the cave was built. It was cheaper to build on a slope, and more costly to build on level ground. It was cheaper to build where ground conditions were favorable, and more expensive where a great deal of earth had to be removed.

4

Also, according to *how* one built. Whether a stone facade was desired or whether a whitewashed brick facade would do.

Mau Pei-hsin's two caves together cost 520 Y. The quarry work and transportation of the cut stone from the quarry to the building site cost 60 Y, the removal of the earth 40 Y, building work 50 Y, carpentry 60 Y. In addition, it had cost 50 Y to feed the building group. But he had a couple of extra cupboards and a work-bench.

The carpenter who made the windows and doors was a professional. He composed the latticework in the window-vault individually for each family. No two new caves in the whole village were alike.

"He wanted each facade to suit its family," said Mau Pei-hsin. "If there is some flower that family is particularly fond of, then he'll make a pattern with just those flowers for them. There must be harmony between a family and the home it is to live in. That's why no two windows are alike here among us. This is nothing that has to be paid for. It's his job. He's paid a daily wage by the brigade, and we who are having the houses built pay for his latticework according to how many windows and doors and cupboards we want to have."

This care over aesthetic matters applied not only to the private construction that was going on, but also, of course, to the brigade's own buildings. In 1962 there had been only a couple of types of lattice. Now—after the cultural revolution—each new building had been given an individual character. Not merely were they building more. They were building more permanently and more beautifully.

There was a building plan now. Each family decides for itself when it wants to build, and how large its home is to be. It is usual to build two stone caves. In only one case has a family built a single cave, in a couple of cases, three. This has been decided by the size of the family.

But it is the business of the Revolutionary Committee to ensure that the site is suitable. "It's better and cheaper to build in rows."

The building is done in a planned fashion. The brigade's building team goes from one village to the next. Stone caves are not only more expensive to build than ordinary caves: they also take longer. They have to stand open and dry out for a whole summer before being plastered. Then they have to dry for two more months before the carpenter can do his work and the family can move in. Only by planning the building work for the brigade as a whole is it possible to work rationally and save building costs.

But the building plan is not decided by the Revolutionary Committee at a closed meeting. It is prepared by general discussion at mass meetings, open to all. Then it is worked over by the Revolutionary Committee, and the final decision is reached only after new and thorough discussions at public mass meetings. In five to ten years from now every household in the brigade will have moved into new stone caves. But stone caves can stand for five hundred years without any extensive renovations being necessary. What is being built today is going to stand a long time. That's why it is so important for everyone to think out the forward planning with great care and express his or her opinion at the meetings.

"We are just working out a detailed plan for this building work," said Feng Chang-yeh, "but before we decide on it we must review our experiences of the last three years as a whole. That is what we are discussing at the moment. We have built according to plan. The directives have been worked out in common for the whole brigade. Today the first families have already been living in this new type of large stone cave for a couple of years. So now is the time to discuss our experiences before deciding on the building plan as a whole."

6

In 1962 drinking water was still a problem. They took water from the brook. Today new wells have been dug and bricked in for drinking water. All the village's households have access to good water. Wang You-nan, the brigade doctor, said it could be drunk without having to be boiled. Yet they still always drink boiled water.

The big loudspeakers had been moved to the schoolyard. The schoolyard is used for meetings and film shows. Tsao Chen-kuei said, "Today virtually every household has a radio of its own. A little transistor or a larger set. So we no longer need a central radio. If we want to summon a meeting of the whole village then we beat on the triangle."

There had been an increase in the number of bicycles and two-wheeled carts (with rubber tires) such as can either be pulled by hand or attached to a bicycle. The standard of clothing had risen. In 1962 they were proud that every villager had winter clothes. Now people had begun changing into better clothes in the evening or to go to meetings.

The "planned distribution" of 1962, which had involved rationing of certain consumer goods, had come to an end, except for cotton. But even here the ration had grown considerably. In 1962 the annual ration (in *Report from a Chinese Village,* p. 68, I give the half-yearly ration) had been 7.4 chi for adults and 10.4 for children. Now it was 17.6 per person a year.

Prices in the Seven-mile Village shop were generally lower than they had been in 1962. Cotton cloth cost 0.28 Y per chi, compared with 0.295 Y per chi in 1962. Rubber shoes had fallen from 4.59 to 4.09 Y, and so forth. Cotton thread and cooking oil were somewhat more expensive than in 1962 (sewing thread 0.77 Y per skein, as against 0.15 Y per skein in 1962). Prices for some goods had fallen sharply. Handkerchiefs had fallen from 0.435 Y to 0.18 Y; vinegar per jin from 0.09 Y to 0.05 Y; stoneware jars holding 80 jin of grain from 9.91 Y to 4.26 Y; water cauldrons (iron) for 20 liters of water from 7.82 to 5.30 Y; bicycles from 178 Y to 145 Y. (A new line in alarm clocks had come in, costing 7.10 Y apiece as against the old alarm clocks which in 1962 had cost 16.30 Y). Spirits 60%, cookies, and candy had all become cheaper.

There were more beehives around the village. The number of household pigs had risen. Each family should now have two pigs. One they ate, and one they sold. The brigade sold the piglets for 5 Y apiece to market, and for 4 Y apiece to members. The State bought the pigs for 50–60 Y apiece when fully reared. The dung was given to the brigade for work-points (100 jin = 1 point).

Now there were ten dogs in the village of Liu Ling. Large, long-haired, good-natured dogs. As far as I could see, these ten pets had no other function than to play with the children, be scratched by their masters and sleep in the sun. There were no stray dogs. (But there were also working dogs. Big sheepdogs. But these were just family dogs.)

It may seem irrelevant to start a book on the cultural revolution in China by talking about house-building, aesthetic window lattices and family dogs.

But it is vital to point out that the standard of living in Liu Ling has risen during the cultural revolution. Propaganda from Moscow and Washington has tried to give the world the impression that Chinese policy is based on people starving themselves. The Pekingologues talk of the cultural revolution as a struggle for power within the Party leadership; have represented it as resulting in a drop in the standard of living. They have talked darkly. Now they are trying to run away from what they said in 1966–67.

The basis of Chinese policy—to use Mao Tse-tung's words: "Serve the People"—is that all of China's hundreds of millions shall attain a better life.

The victory in the Chinese Revolution cost great sacrifices. (The old people at Liu Ling could tell me about that; see *Report from a Chinese Village*.) But victory had only been possible that time, in 1949, because the Chinese Communist Party had fought a people's war. Mao Tsetung, describing the relationship between the revolutionary war and the prosperity of the masses at the Second National Congress of Workers' and Peasants' Representatives at Jui-chin on January 27, 1934, said:

Our central task at present is to mobilize the broad masses to take part in the revolutionary war, overthrow imperialism and the Kuomintang by means of such war, spread the revolution throughout the country, and drive imperialism out of China. Anyone who does not attach enough importance to this central task is not a good revolutionary cadre. If our comrades really comprehend this task and understand that the revolution must at all costs be spread throughout the country, then they should in no way neglect or underestimate the question of the immediate interests, the well-being, of the broad masses. For the revolutionary war is a war of the masses; it can be waged only by mobilizing the masses and relying on them. . . .

I earnestly suggest to this congress that we pay close attention to the well-being of the masses, from the problems of land and labor to those of fuel, rice, cooking oil and salt. The women want to learn plowing and harrowing. Whom can we get to teach them? The children want to go to school. Have we set up primary schools? The wooden bridge over there is too narrow and people may fall off. Should we not repair it? Many people suffer from boils and other ailments. What are we going to do about it? All such problems concerning the well-being of the masses should be placed on our agenda. We should discuss them, adopt and carry out decisions and check up on the results.

The Politics of a Threshing Machine

The great discussion in China's countryside about "the two lines" has not been a discussion between the protagonists of a "better life" (private consumption) and the protagonists of a "lower standard of living" (collective investment). What the cultural revolutionaries have pointed out is that the very condition for "a better life" is collective investment.

The issue is not really a strange one. Take a concrete example: The threshing machine. Formerly, threshing was done by flails, and oxen had been used to trample out the grain. At the annual meeting at the beginning of 1969, threshing was discussed. Threshing took a long time. It consumed a lot of labor. The electrician, Mau Pei-hsin, proposed that a threshing machine should be bought. After all, there was now an electrical supply. This purchase would mean less cash income for the brigade members.

"On an average it is going to cost us 3 Y each this year." But a threshing machine would make the work easier and raise production. It would release a great deal of labor.

After a detailed discussion the meeting decided unanimously to buy the threshing machine and take the purchase money from funds which otherwise should have been distributed among the members. The threshing machine was bought. Now, in the autumn of 1969, it was running day and night.

This cannot be represented as a fight between "private consumption" and "collective investment." The meeting regarded collective investment as the condition of higher yield and therefore of a higher standard of living.

Seven years ago all the grain had been ground by the women by hand or at the donkey-driven mill. This was heavy work. It took a long time. It was wearisome. Now the millstones at the big donkey-mill were deeply sunk in the ground. The mill is no longer in use. The little hand mills are only used exceptionally when it is suddenly necessary to grind very small quantities. The brigade had built a mill house (a large stone cave) with electric mills. Here the households also did their own milling. Li Yang-ching's household consisted of seven persons. They consumed about 1,500 kg. of grain a year. Formerly she used to grind all this herself, by hand. Now it was being ground for her in the brigade mill.

The brigade charges at cost for this service. The prices vary slightly for different sorts of grain. On an average it is 0.66 Y per 100 kg. of grain. Last year Li Yang-ching paid about 10 Y. This is deducted from the money she gets for her work. But since the mill has freed her—as it has the other women—from the hardest and most time-consuming part of her household work, and this has given her more time for agriculture, so her working income has risen.

During these years there had been big investments in the brigade. For building, acquiring machinery, laying out terraces. "Before the cultural revolution," said Feng Chang-yeh, "it could happen that we had to ask for a loan from the People's Commune or the State. Nowadays we make all our investments with our own work and our own capital. This is the result of our having studied Mao Tse-tung's thought. We have learned from Tachai."

The bank loan which the brigade had in 1962—4,000 Y—was paid off in 1965. Since then nothing has been borrowed either from the People's Commune or from the State.

11

"Major expenditure," said Feng Chang-yeh, "has to be approved by the Revolutionary Committee of the People's Commune. For instance, the building of stone caves for the brigade. For only one or two such caves we don't have to go to the People's Commune; but when whole rows of them are in question, then the investment has to be approved by the Commune. This is also true of the purchase of machinery, threshing machines, mills and so forth. Also such projects as the noodle factory have to be approved. But the People's Commune itself hasn't carried out any major projects during these last few years."

The village has been transformed. It looks different. There are many newly built rows of caves. Production, too, has risen. The brigade's grain output, which in 1961 was 160 tons, had risen by 1965 to 240 tons, and the 1969 harvest was estimated at 325 tons. The area of arable ground had not increased; but terraces had been laid out, wells dug, the irrigated area increased, and more fertilizer laid out. In 1962, when we left Liu Ling, they gave us four apples. It was their first apple harvest. In 1969, 50 tons of apples were sold to the State. Vegetable produce had risen to 300 tons, at the same time as the area had grown smaller (but the amount of fertilizer used had grown vastly). The brigade's collective funds now amounted to 160,000 Y and an emergency store had been created (against war, natural catastrophes or crop failure). The emergency store amounted at present to 75 tons of grain. Was to be increased.

So—what had happened at Liu Ling?

Study Meeting

The evening of October 18 was fixed for the regular bi-weekly study meeting of the Poor and Lower Middle Peasants Associations' members in the Fourth and Fifth Labor Groups (which in 1962 had been called the Liu-Ling Village Labor Group and Hutoma Village Labor Group). The meeting was to be held in the stone cave of the Swineherds beside the animal shed, below the noodle factory.

The meeting was to commence at 7:00 P.M. But it was raining and the ground was slippery. It was quite a while before everyone had turned up. While waiting for the others, people sat on the kang, smoked and chatted. As the participants gradually turned up they packed themselves closer together to make room. Everyone had brought *Quotations from Chairman Mao Tse-tung*. When all had assembled, the chairman of the meeting, Fu Hai-tsao, got up and declared the meeting open, and proposed that it should begin with the *Song of the Helmsman*. He struck up the tune, and everyone else joined in.

> *Sailing the seas depends on the helmsman,*
> *All living things depend on the sun for their*
> *   growth,*
> *Moistened by rain and dew, young crops grow*
> *   strong,*
> *Making revolution depends on the thought of Mao*
> *   Tse-tung.*
>
> *Fish can't live without water,*
> *Melons can't thrive off their vine,*

13

The revolutionary masses cannot do without the
  Communist Party,
Mao Tse-tung's thought is the never-setting sun.

The chairman proposed that they begin with the first quotation of the first chapter in their books. And everyone read in chorus:

The force at the core leading our cause forward is the Chinese Communist Party. The theoretical basis guiding our thinking is Marxism-Leninism.

The chairman proposed that the second quotation of the nineteenth chapter be read. And everyone read in chorus:

Give full play to our style of fighting—courage in battle, no fear of sacrifice, no fear of fatigue, and continuous fighting (that is fighting successive battles in a short time without rest).

The chairman proposed that they read the fourth quotation of the nineteenth chapter. And everyone read in chorus:

Be resolute, fear no sacrifice and surmount every difficulty to win victory.

The chairman says that today we are to study "The Foolish Old Man Who Removed the Mountains" (Mao Tse-tung's concluding speech at the Party Congress in 1945), and gives the word to the leader of studies.

The study leader (Li Chi-shen, 24 years, son of Li Haitsai, has gone through middle school at Yenan, is now teacher at Liu Yang school) begins to read. He reads slowly and clearly. Now and again he interrupts his reading to explain words, phrases and signs:

There is an ancient Chinese fable called "The Foolish Old Man Who Removed the Mountains." It tells of an old man who lived in northern China long, long ago and was known as the Foolish Old Man of North Mountain. His house faced south and beyond his doorway stood the two great peaks, Taihang and Wangwu, obstructing the way. He called his sons, and hoe in hand they began to dig up these mountains with great determination. Another greybeard, known as the Wise Old Man, saw them and said derisively, "How silly of you to do this! It is quite impossible for you few to dig up these two huge mountains." The Foolish Old Man replied, "When I die, my sons will carry on; when they die, there will be my grandsons, and then their sons and grandsons, and so on to infinity. High as they are, the mountains cannot grow any higher and with every bit we dig, they will be that much lower. Why can't we clear them away?" Having refuted the Wise Old Man's wrong view, he went on digging every day, unshaken in his conviction. God was moved by this, and he sent down two angels, who carried the mountains away on their backs. Today, two big mountains lie like a dead weight on the Chinese people. One is imperialism, the other is feudalism. The Chinese Communist Party has long made up its mind to dig them up. We must persevere and work unceasingly, and we, too, will touch God's heart. Our God is none other than the masses of the Chinese people. If they stand up and dig together with us, why can't these two mountains be cleared away?

The chairman says that the most serious questions just now concern the autumn harvest. He says anyone may speak.

Ma Juei-ching says the rains are extraordinarily heavy. This rain is a threat to the harvest. But at the same time they mustn't forget to start work, soon, on the soil-improvement and anti-erosion schemes.

Wang Yu-lan says that the work is often begun too late in the morning. There is also too much grain spilled on the way.

Li Hai-yuan says they must remember Chairman Mao's words:

15

Be prepared against war, be prepared against natural disasters, and do everything for the people.

The grain is necessary.

Tsao Ming-wa says too much has in fact been wasted in transport. Every grain must be saved. Attention must be paid to this.

Wang Yu-hua refers to what Chairman Mao has said: "Fear neither difficulties nor death." One must serve the people and work for the revolution. So it is right to start earlier in the mornings during harvest-time. Each grain of corn is precious.

Li Hai-kuei says that what has been said is right. Time must be put to better use. For now the fruits of a whole year's hard work are being harvested.

Li Hai-chun says that the result of a thorough study of "The Foolish Old Man who Removed the Mountains" would be a record harvest.

Li Hai-ching says that Chairman Mao's words:

"Be resolute, fear no sacrifice and surmount every difficulty to win victory,"

have inspired the Labor Group to do its utmost. Grain is valuable and the harvest will be good. It is also necessary to save every grain and not let the harvest be wasted.

Fu Ai-ying challenges all the women to become more active and contribute more during harvest-time.

Ai Ta-ping says all the women must take this seriously.

Feng Chang-yeh says the question of soil-improvement and reducing erosion has to be discussed as well as that of the harvesting. This is very important. His view is that one-third of the labor force should be detailed off for it.

The chairman asks whether one-third of the labor force for soil-improvement and combating erosion is a proper proportion.

Various voices say that one-third is right.

Feng Chang-yeh says that there are now only four days of harvest work left. The time must be used well. Thus, he agrees with the comrades who have said they must start earlier in the mornings during these days.

The chairman asks whether everyone is in agreement about this.

The meeting agrees unanimously.

Feng Chang-yeh says a decision has already been reached as to how the plowed fields down in the valley are to be embanked. But they must also bear in mind the terracing and anti-erosion work. He doesn't want to raise the question as a whole. Merely asks everyone to bear it in mind. It must be discussed. But in the next few days what is vital is to harvest the beans and kaoliang.

The chairman asks whether the meeting can now be closed. Thereafter he suggests they read the fourth quotation of the nineteenth chapter. Everyone reads in chorus:

Be resolute, fear no sacrifice and surmount every difficulty to win victory.

The chairman proposes that the meeting shall close by singing the *Song of the Helmsman*. He begins to sing, and everyone else joins in. The meeting is at an end; everyone goes home. It is still raining. Here and there one can see people lighting their way with pocket flashlights.

Clarification

In 1962 I filled column after column at Liu Ling with figures. These were to help clarify what was going on. To explain what had been happening during the seven years since then, such a method was impractical for several reasons.

In several cases I this time, for security reasons, was refused concrete information. Tsao Chen-kuei, who was now responsible for the People's Militia, said, "Since the winter of 1962–63 the People's Militia's weapons are in the village. We keep our weapons in our homes."

Who had these weapons, how they trained, what results had been achieved, how the People's Militia is currently organized, were questions Tsao Chen-kuei refused to answer: "I don't want to tell you. These are internal matters, they concern only ourselves. But I can tell you that we are following Chairman Mao's instructions:

Be prepared against war, be prepared against natural disasters, and do everything for the people.

And

The imperialists are bullying us in such a way that we will have to deal with them seriously. Not only must we have a powerful regular army, we must also organize contingents of the people's militia on a big scale. This will make it difficult for the imperialists to move a single inch in our country in the event of invasion.

In all our work we have taken Mao Tse-tung thought as our guide. Work in the People's Militia, like all other work, is guided by the great principle 'grasp revolution, promote production and other work and preparedness against war.' As for figures and details and concrete information on our defense work, I cannot give you any. You must understand."

(It should be pointed out, perhaps, that the People's Liberation Army had no base in the neighborhood, there were no "military zones" in the brigade from which we were excluded. Gun moved about perfectly freely everywhere, without having anyone accompany her or being supervised. For my part, I mostly sat in the cave and interviewed people.)

This refusal to give any information about military dispositions is perfectly natural. It comprised information on economic defense and the measures taken by the State.

But these years of the cultural revolution had also brought about a change in the entire administration. Many of the figures I was able to obtain in 1962 were now difficult to come by. There was no longer anyone whose business it was to write down such things.

"You can go around and ask for yourself," said Tsao Chen-kuei.

"The Revolutionary Committee can't help you," said Feng Chang-yeh. "The simple fact of the matter is, we don't keep such statistics any longer."

This is correct. In other chapters of this book it will appear that the administration has been simplified and changed in such a way that no further records were being kept about many of the facts I was able to obtain in 1962. I can accept that it is more important to simplify administration than to keep a team of accountants at the beck and call of visiting foreigners.

A third difficulty was that the leading cadres had no right to give concrete information on future work, plans, or goals on their own. The masses must decide. Tung Yang-chen said, "It's hard to say anything about our future work. Just now the masses are discussing what our tasks are to be. This discussion is not yet over. The masses still haven't decided. That's why I can't make any statements."

Feng Chang-yeh explained the situation as follows: "Formerly, before the cultural revolution, I thought the masses at Liu Ling were stupid. After all, I knew best what needed to be done. And I told them. But I thought they didn't understand. They wouldn't pay proper attention. I thought I knew best. If only they did what I told them, everything would be all right. It was for their own good, I thought. After all, they didn't understand as much as we, their leaders, did. We could survey things. We understood how they hung together. That's what I thought—then. During the cultural revolution I was much criticized for this. After the masses' criticism of me and others and after the great criticism against Liu Shao-ch'i I began to realize I'd been wrong in setting myself up above the masses. I became self-critical. It would have been wrong of me to give orders and not listen to what the masses themselves had to say. Now we no longer give orders. Now I don't try to teach the masses lessons and tell them what they're to do. Now we take up problems at study meetings. And solve them there. This is a big change."

The individuals who made these statements were people I'd known since 1962. People I'd associated with. I could discuss things with them. To have gained any idea of what had happened in Liu Ling would have been hard, not to say impossible, had I only spoken to the young Party Vice-Secretary, Liu Teh-ching. Last time I was at Liu Ling I had not met her. At that time she lived in the village of Hutoma. Now she was a member of the Liu Ling Revolutionary Committee. To my question of how the Revolutionary Committee made up its budgets, she replied, "I've forgotten."

When I asked her about the families' incomes, she replied, "That's of no importance. I don't think about money."

When I asked Tsao Chen-kuei how this could be, he said, "In a way she's right. She doesn't know much about the brigade's economic work. She's responsible for propaganda and her contacts go outwards. Her work doesn't have to do with our economy."

I can understand Liu Teh-ching. I can also explain her attitude politically. One works for the revolution. This was something many pointed out. It had been one of the main questions during the discussions of the cultural revolution. But the same question which got me such a tart answer from Liu Teh-ching and her statement that she didn't think about money, and that anyone asking about such matters merely showed he was too interested in trifles, brought quite another answer from Chang Chung-liang: "In our family we are just now discussing whether we should build ourselves some stone caves. In 1967 we bought a bicycle and a cart with rubber tires. That took all our savings. Now we have saved 250 Y. But that's not enough to start building. But if we save for another year we should be able to afford it. I think we'll be able to start building in about a year from now."

The difference between these answers was not that Chang Chung-liang was being "egotistic" or merely "thinking of money." On the contrary, Liu Teh-ching explained that she wanted to ". . . learn from Chang Chung-liang. He has shown great unselfishness. When we had a severe winter he took from his own savings to give extra grain to the animals. He gave away 2,000 jin of grain out of his own store. I want to learn from his example, how to serve the collective and the revolution with all my heart."

Chang Chung-liang himself hadn't told me that story. I only heard it from others. Liu Teh-ching was a young girl who was still living at home with her parents. Chang

Chung-liang was an adult, a family father. That made a certain difference. But so, certainly, did I. He knew me from 1962. She didn't. They reacted differently to my work in the village.

This is something that must not be forgotten. As best I can, I am trying to give an account of what has been happening in a village in northern Shensi. But it must be taken for what it is. An account. A repetition, with explanations, of what people told me.

Transformation

The administrative structure which had been built up in Liu Ling up to 1962 was a complex one (see, *inter alia,* Feng Chang-yeh's account in *Report from a Chinese Village*). Representation and management; control committee and accounts; clearly distinguished functions. In 1962, it's true, the "Old Secretary" was still unquestionably the leading personality; but young, energetic—and literate—men had begun to rise to administrative positions. This meant that old—illiterate—peasants who had taken part in the revolution from the very beginning were now being replaced by people whose real merits were that they knew how to read and keep accounts.

During the cultural revolution this structure had been transformed into a unified and directly elected management: the Revolutionary Committee, which worked under permanent supervision from public meetings and public discussion. Accountancy had been simplified. It was being done in people's spare time. It was not rewarded with any work-points. At Liu Ling—as all over China—Mao Tse-tung's advice to simplify all administration and remove unnecessary regulations and rules were being followed.

Yet in Liu Ling there had been no unified bureaucracy, no real officials, in the true meaning of the word, in 1962. But the cadres had begun to free themselves from production and from the masses' control. This course of events was hastened by the decreasing physical strength of the Old Secretary during 1963. When, in 1964, the Old

Secretary fell seriously ill, more and more of his responsibilities were taken over by younger, literate persons; and when, in August of 1965, he finally died of cancer of the stomach, Feng Chang-yeh succeeded to the post of Party Secretary and greatly reduced his productive working hours.

The process was automatic. It was no conscious or planned distortion of Mao Tse-tung's policy for the masses. But it found its theoretical expression in Liu Shao-ch'i's talk about the low cultural level out in the villages. It made it quite natural for the cadres—who were conscious of having had more schooling—to begin "deciding on their own" because they "knew better." There was nothing strange about this. But over the years it came to have political and economic consequences.

In 1962 Li Hsiu-tang had bowed in a friendly way every time Gun or I met him. His children went on to receive higher education. He was to be Lo Han-hong's father-in-law, Lo Han-hong being the accountant and secretary of the Youth League. His cave was the finest in the whole village. But the Old Secretary said, "I know him inside out." And Mau Ke-yeh said, "He is the only real counter-revolutionary we have here in the village. If he should ever show that he works hard and has become a new person, then he will get his civil rights back. But he hasn't shown any signs of that yet. Of course, his father owned many thousand mu here." But the young Tsao Chen-kuei, at that time vice-chairman of the brigade board of management, a Party member responsible for agricultural work, who wrote for newspapers and other journals, just said, "People talk such a lot." It was in that year Mao Tse-tung exhorted the Communists never to forget class struggle.

Things had been going much the same way all over China. The cadres had begun to turn into bureaucrats. They were telling themselves the people didn't understand much. The newly-overthrown landowner class had begun to make connections, to marry into the cadres, smile pleasantly, and bow. Their children were going on to receive higher education, getting higher marks. As for the class struggle, the young cadres were beginning to say, "People talk such a lot!"

Economic policy, too, had begun to change. It was beginning to be regarded as self-evident that some sort of piece-work system was more "efficient."

All this has been settled by the cultural revolution. It had taken a long time. The cultural revolution, it is important to bear in mind, was not a sudden change: a struggle lasting only a few days or weeks. At Liu Ling the Revolutionary Committee was not formed until two years and five weeks after the Central Committee had pointed out in its decision concerning the Great Proletarian Cultural Revolution of August 8, 1966, that

> It is necessary to institute a system of general elections, like that of the Paris Commune, for electing members to the cultural revolutionary groups and committees, and delegates to the cultural revolutionary congresses. The lists of candidates should be put forward by the revolutionary masses after full discussion, and the elections should be held after the masses have discussed the lists over and over again.
>
> The masses are entitled at any time to criticize members of the cultural revolutionary groups and committees and delegates elected to the cultural revolutionary congresses. If these members or delegates prove incompetent, they can be replaced through election or recalled by the masses after discussion.
>
> —— From the ninth point of the decision: "Cultural Revolutionary Groups, Committees and Congresses"

These two years had been characterized by continuous political discussion. The Revolutionary Committee was not formed as a result of a purely formal decision. It was

25

the outcome of a long revolutionary process of discussion and criticism.

The cultural revolution had been preceded by criticism —which had been silenced—from older revolutionaries. It had continued with criticism from members of the Youth League. They had been reading Mao Tse-tung and had begun to say to the cadres, "What you're doing doesn't agree with the words of Chairman Mao." When the Red Guards arrived, in the autumn of 1966, and spread the little red book: *Quotations from Chairman Mao Tse-tung,* the major criticism gained force.

At Liu Ling two groups had initiated the cultural revolution: the literate and politically active youngsters who compared the words of Mao with what was really going on in the village, and the old poor peasants and early Communists. These groups had gathered everyone in the brigade to a discussion to present their criticisms. Those who formed the vanguard of the cultural revolution were organized Communists: veterans and youngsters.

The cultural revolution was no quarrel over the pope's beard or the donkey's shadow. Nor a matter of subtle nuances. The points at issue were basic. Questions directly concerning everyone. That persons in leading positions were attacked and criticized did not mean they were regarded as enemies. Feng Chang-yeh had been the chairman of the brigade and, since 1965, secretary of the brigade party organization. He had been criticized for following wrong directives from above and for beginning to behave like a bureaucrat. He himself said he had been on a dangerous path. During those long discussions he changed his attitude. When the Revolutionary Committee was formed, on September 15, 1968, he was elected chairman.

The cultural revolution was no struggle for power over key positions. Mau Pei-hsin was the first person to put up a big-character poster in the village. A direct attack

26

on Feng Chang-yeh, it accused him of neglecting Chairman Mao's instructions, of following an erroneous economic policy and of behaving like a bureaucrat.

Mau Pei-hsin was the son of Mau Ke-yeh. Mau Pei-hsin had joined the Youth League in 1949, had become a Party member in 1952. He was an electrician. On the orders of the Party he returned to the village in 1965 to do political work and help mechanize agriculture. Politically, he was one of the most active people in the village. And had been throughout the cultural revolution. In the evenings of 1969 the young people of the village gathered in his cave to discuss politics. But he had not struggled against Feng Chang-yeh just to get himself an important position. The cultural revolution had not meant that the village simply exchanged Feng for Mau. What it led to was a change in policy. And to Feng and Mau finally reaching unity.

When the Cultural Revolution Reached the Village

Liu Teh-ching:

"In the summer of 1962 I finished school at Liu Ling. Then I began working in the Hutoma Village Labor Group. My father was working there too. In January 1964 I became a member of the Youth League. At that time Li Hai-tsai was its secretary. That was the year when Mao Tse-tung told us to learn from Tachai. We studied the three constantly read articles: ('In Memory of Norman Bethune,' 'Serve the People,' and 'The Foolish Old Man Who Removed the Mountains'). We also studied Liu Shao-ch'i. We thought he used some strange expressions. Mao Tse-tung was much easier to understand. For example 'Serve the People.' That's very easily understood.

"At Liu Ling a very sharp fight developed between the two lines. We followed Mao's exhortation to learn from Tachai, but the situation here at Liu Ling didn't accord with that at Tachai. The collective economy was being undermined. We did not criticize Liu Shao-ch'i's line. But we criticized concrete phenomena which seemed to us wrong in the light of Mao Tse-tung's thinking. The private plots of land were getting larger. Work-points were being turned into piece-work. We also criticized the tendency to ignore the class struggle. Some of our comrades here at Liu Ling imagined the class struggle was over. We held power now, and the class enemy, they believed, would no longer dare to oppose the people. Certain comrades drew no clear distinction between themselves and the class enemy. They had friendly contacts with Li Hsiu-tang. Associated with him. Talked with him. We criticized them for this. We also criticized Li

Hung-fu for neglecting his political work and Li Hai-tsai for his proneness to get angry with folk and bawl them out. But all this criticism was made internally at joint meetings of the Youth League and the Party organization. We didn't take our criticism to the masses. Nor did we try to rouse the masses to criticize the cadres.

"Then, in 1964, we read Mao Tse-tung. But it would be wrong to say we studied Mao Tse-tung Thought. We thought such studies were something for older people only. But in 1965 I was at a meeting of the Youth League at Yenan. There I was given *Quotations from Chairman Mao Tse-tung*. It was an edition printed for the People's Liberation Army. At that time the book of quotations was not generally available.

"The 'Three Constantly-Read Articles' had been easy. Yet they contained difficulties. And to study the works of Chairman Mao would really have been very difficult. From all those volumes it would have by no means been easy to select the main ideas. But the conference emphasized how important it was to study Mao Tse-tung Thought, and to bring up young people in its light. The quotations made it much easier to grasp the main ideas. This was how it really became possible to spread the study of Mao Tse-tung Thought.

"It was at the end of the winter of 1965 I came home from that conference. I had the book of quotations with me. It was the only copy in the whole brigade. We discussed how to spread it. We decided to multiply the most important quotations and spread them in the brigade. We printed sheets of paper with the quotations. And spread them. And we were still doing it when the cultural revolution began; yes, and went on doing so until the book of quotations had come out in big editions and been spread to every member of the brigade.

"It was in June, 1966, I first heard anyone speak of the cultural revolution. To begin with I didn't understand it

29

fully. Like others in our Youth League, I thought it was something that had only to do with art and literature. Not until the summer did we understand what the cultural revolution was all about. Then we followed Chairman Mao's exhortations

'grasp revolution, promote production'

and,

'you must concern yourselves with state affairs and carry the great proletarian cultural revolution through to the end.'"

Hsueh Si-chun:

"I began school at Liu Ling when I was eighteen. That was in 1953. I'd not been to school before. I came from a poor peasant's home. Things had been hard for us. But in 1953 I decided to study. For four years I attended Liu Ling School. But I was poisoned by the pernicious influence of Liu Shao-ch'i. I'd begun to study to become an official. I wanted to get better work in town or in the administration. When I got back to my village after finishing school in 1957, I was disappointed. I didn't want to work on agriculture. After all, I'd studied, hadn't I? But anyway, I began working on the land. I became an ordinary agricultural worker.

"I was an ordinary member of the commune and held no position. Nor was I a Party member. In the autumn of 1964 I was publicly criticized at a meeting. They said I was lazy and that I tried to get out of doing the heaviest work. They said I was selfish. I took this very much to heart.

"I wanted to correct my mistakes and improve. I thought a lot about this. After all, I was a poor peasant. But the criticism had been right. Then I heard on the radio about studying Mao Tse-tung Thought. I heard people talking about activists who had overcome difficulties and improved and achieved results by studying Mao Tse-tung Thought. But the brigade leadership was doing nothing to spread Mao Tse-tung Thought. Nor was the leadership of the commune doing anything. In May, 1965, I was at Yenan. I went to the bookshop. And there I bought brochures by Mao Tse-tung. I took them home and began to read them and found they were very important. Mao Tse-tung answered all my questions. When I read about Chang Szu-teh and how wholeheartedly he had served the people, and when I read about Norman Bethune and how, even though he came from Canada, he had died for the people of China, I was inspired to overcome my own faults and work harder. All that year I studied Mao Tse-tung Thought."

Tsao Chen-kuei:

"We'd made many mistakes in the brigade leadership. We hadn't put politics first. We hadn't urged the masses to study Mao Tse-tung Thought. That's why Hsueh Si-chun's initiative achieved such importance. In February, 1966, there was to be a big conference at Yenan. Those who had been active in studying Mao Tse-tung Thought were to gather. We discussed this in the brigade leadership and called a meeting. We asked who was an activist. Then everyone said Hsueh Si-chun was. He was chosen to go to the conference at Yenan. At that meeting we urged the masses to learn from Hsueh Si-chun. But we didn't do much more. We did nothing to organize studies. All we did was to urge people to read Mao Tse-tung's writings."

Hsueh Si-chun:

"The board of the brigade urged the masses to learn from me, and then, in the spring of 1966, many began to buy

31

brochures with Mao Tse-tung's works and study them. There were a great many things I found wrong in the brigade. I read Mao Tse-tung and found people in the brigade were not acting according to his ideas. But I didn't dare come out with my criticism. After all, I was only an ordinary member. Even if I read Mao Tse-tung, and even if I understood that things weren't as they should be in the brigade, I didn't dare revolt. Being only an ordinary member I thought it wasn't for me to criticize the leadership.

"According to Chairman Mao the cadres ought to serve the people wholeheartedly. But in the brigade the great thing was work-points. That didn't accord with what Chairman Mao had said! He who wants to serve the people mustn't separate himself from the masses for a single instant, but the leaders of the brigade didn't take part in any manual work. They sat in their offices and were becoming bureaucrats. All this I thought. But I said nothing out loud.

"Not until the Red Guards arrived did things change. The Red Guards came to spread Mao Tse-tung Thought. I was appointed to work on the reception committee. There were many practical problems to be solved. The Red Guards influenced me. We discussed a great deal. They said that everything that didn't accord with Mao Tse-tung Thought must go. Act like Chairman Mao, they said. Don't be afraid. Then I plucked up courage and rebelled and criticized the bourgeois ideas."

Kao Pin-ying:

"In those years it was a hard struggle between the two lines. Right up to 1965, the private lots of land were on the increase. Some people got higher incomes, some lower. But in 1965 discussion started in earnest. In these discussions the members of the commune said that if we

32

continued along the way we had begun to follow we'd be on the way to revisionism. We learned from Tachai and altered course. We cut down the private lots."

Feng Chang-yeh:

"It was in the spring of 1965 the brigade took up the whole question. We should learn from Tachai. The party organization organized big meetings. At them we discussed the question of the private lots."

Kao Pin-ying:

"When the Red Guards came in August I heard people talking about the cultural revolution. They had come to learn from us. They came to spread the cultural revolution. The Red Guards lived in my cave too. They gave a hand with the household work and paid their way. They asked me about my life. They also talked about the situation in Peking. They discussed China's future with me. The Soviet Union had followed the path of revisionism. If we didn't carry through the cultural revolution we should infallibly do the same. Among us, too, there were renegades, even among the leadership. Even at that time, August, 1966, there were some Red Guards from Peking who mentioned Liu Shao-ch'i's name when they talked to me. They told me various things. My first thought was that if there were traitors to the revolution in the government of the whole country, then there must be some lower down too. They must have their people in the province, at Yenan, in the People's Commune. During these conversations with the Red Guards I and others found a clean-up was necessary. So we threw ourselves into the cultural revolution."

The village has 37 households. It is the seat of the Liu Ling Brigade. The brigade has 161 households; 709 inhabitants, of whom 301 work. Liu Ling lies in the northern Shensi loess country. The soil of the valley is fertile; but most of the

BELOW: Wang Shih-chieh, age 20;

RIGHT: Liu Chen-yung, age 37

plowed fields lie on the slopes of hills. In 1961, total grain output was 160 tons. In 1969, it was estimated at 325 tons. Also 50 tons of apples and 300 tons of vegetables. During the cultural revolution half the village's inhabitants have built new stone caves. The tractor is made in China and belongs to the Machine and Tractor Station at Yenan.

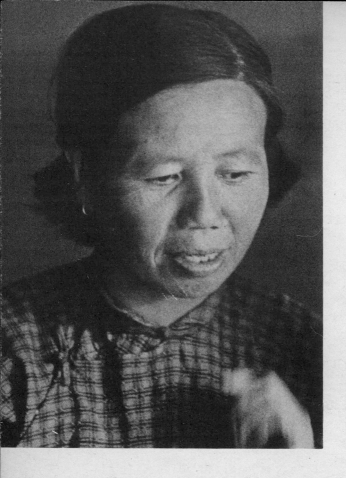

ABOVE:
Li Yang-ching, age 36

TOP RIGHT:
Liu Shao-lu, a boy, age 7
Liu Lan-shuan, a girl, age 16, Seventh Class

BOTTOM RIGHT:
Liu Lian-hong, a boy, age 2
Liu Lan-fang, a girl, age 11, Fourth Class
Liu Lu-wa, a boy, age 9, Second Class

Seven years ago they used to say of Li Yang-ching:
"She loves a chat and jokes a lot. . . . She is very orderly and knowledgeable, though there isn't anyone of the older generation in her home. Everything in her cave is well looked after, and her children are well brought up and she works hard. She does more than other women. Most other women stop working in the fields when they have their first child and don't find the day long enough even to look after the children; but she does work in the fields and sees to her home and the children, and has time to chat with her friends and run her home properly."

Of Liu Chen-yung, people said in 1962: "Her husband Liu Chen-yung, is good. Most men here, or at least half of them, anyway, go straight to the kang and lie down and sleep when they get home from work; but he helps her and does things in the home. He is calm, quiet and doesn't speak much. They never quarrel; everyone considers them a happy family."
Even at that time he was a member of the Chinese Communist Party, had been since 1955, but had never had any position in the Party or the collective.

After seven years they were still themselves. He taciturn; she talkative and laughing. Now they had five children. The four older ones looked after the smallest. Their home was tidy. He and she were working, the one as hard as the other. Neither of them was elected to any posts. They were respected and regarded as a happy family.

It was a perfectly ordinary family. But there is nothing derogatory in the word ordinary. They were just two of the many millions of ordinary people whose daily work is shaping history. Generally speaking, this family differed little from the Smiths in Liverpool, or the Joneses in Chicago.

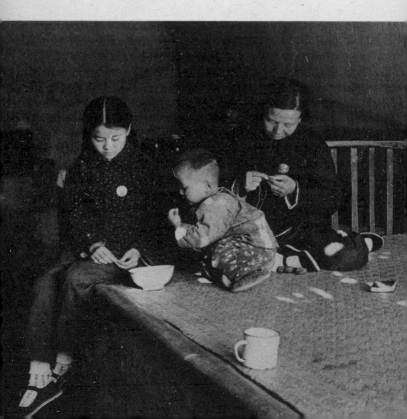

He was a herdsman now. In December, 1966, he was appointed to the job. At the meeting various jobs had been discussed. It was thought that he had a good hand with animals, he was orderly in his ways. So he was appointed herdsman.

In the morning he goes with the animals. As soon as the paths up the hillside have had time to dry out and the dew is gone, he's on his way. He comes home at sunset. In the household he fetches water from the well, chops wood, sweeps the yard. In the evenings he likes to knit. Here it is the men who knit.

She looks after the household and works in the fields. In 1968 she did 220 days' work in agriculture. When she is out working and the older children are at school, the seven-year-old looks after the youngest. Now the seven-year-old is to begin school. Then the neighbors will look after the smallest boy. That's no problem; people help each other.

45

They have five children. That's enough. They've discussed the question and come to the conclusion that five children are enough.

Last year the family began building two stone caves. They had been standing drying for a year. Now the carpentry work had started. If all the costs are added up, the new home will have cost 600 Y. But that includes everything: carpentry, installation of electricity, everything.

The brigade does all the building. That team goes from village to village, building several stone caves at a time. Afterwards the neighbors help each other with various jobs. There's a lot to be done. But people help each other. This time you help someone else; next time it's you who are helped.

The old dwelling—it wasn't all that old, built in 1961—was to be retained by the family as a storehouse.

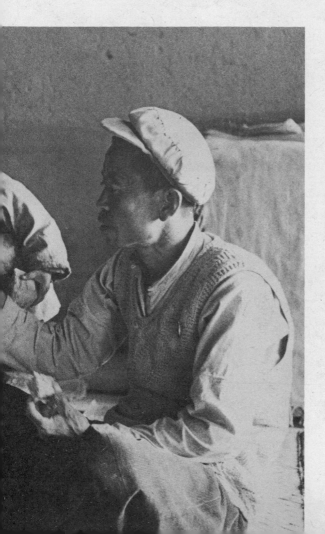

They had saved up for their new home. She had bred up two pigs a year. One of them was eaten by the family; the other was sold to the State. This yielded an extra income of 50–60 Y a year. This money they had not touched; they had kept it for the new dwelling.

"Yes," he said, "this is important, all this building we've done these last few years. And it isn't only people who've got new houses, either. The animals, too, have got proper stone sheds. The new pig-sties, both the big one which is being built down in the valley and the sties up here, the new stable, the new barn; today everything's being properly built of stone."

They had joined in the big discussions which took place during the cultural revolution. She had criticized the cadres. They'd been turning into bureaucrats. They'd begun to have reservations about working in the fields, had been sitting by themselves, deciding things and giving orders. The officials hadn't bothered to study Chairman Mao. But they weren't bad. After criticism they'd improved.

As a Party member he had helped to arrange many meetings. When the cultural revolution began, the Party organization held no closed meetings. After all, the whole idea was to mobilize the masses and get them to speak their minds."

Formerly, neither he nor she could read. Now their daughter Liu Lan-shuan has taught them to read the little red book. That was in the spring of 1967. Their daughter said everyone had to study; she would teach them to read.

Now the whole family studies the words of Chairman Mao twice a week. The daughter teaches her parents what she has learned in school. She explains the meaning of the characters, teaches them to read them, after which they discuss how to act according to Chairman Mao's ideas.

"We must apply what we learn. If we don't, then we haven't learned anything," says their daughter.

In 1962 he and she had helped each other with the housework. This had been regarded as a good thing. They were a young couple. He stayed at home and looked after the children on the evening of October 26 while she took part in the brigade meeting. During the cultural revolution the women had insisted on being allowed to go to meetings. In 1967 they had forced through the adoption of the principle that women should have the same right as men to go to meetings. Not merely the same formal right, either, but the same right in practice. On evenings when the women went, the men should be obliged to look after the children.

"It's good for men to learn how to look after children. In the old days it used to be the men who did all the talking at the meetings. The women had to stay at home and look after the children. Now, since the men have learned how to look after children, the women speak too about state affairs."

The Revolution and People's Welfare

"On the whole," said Li Hai-yuan, "the work-leaders pay more attention now since the cultural revolution, to the experienced farmers. I work in the Fourth Labor Group. I'm still only an ordinary member. It's best to be that. But even if one isn't a work-leader, one can show how things can be done by real hand work. Now the work-leaders are more considerate of us older workers. They don't give us heavy work to do. And then, we hold meetings about everything. At them we discuss the work which has to be done, in detail. Discuss questions of manure and sowing. Today, no one just gives orders any more.

"When one has begun to get old and has a sick wife and no children to support one, it feels good to know that the five guarantees exist," said Li Hai-yuan. He was fifty-five now, and had begun to suffer from bad health.

The "five guarantees" mean that everyone in the collective is guaranteed enough food, enough clothes, enough fuel, an honorable funeral and education for his children.

This was a result of the institution of the People's Commune in 1958. The People's Commune didn't only mean simplified administration and a broader democracy; it also gave greater security. In 1962, Feng Chang-yeh had said, "Illness, death, and accident are no longer catastrophes. Citizens now have security."

It was the collective—no longer the family or clan—that had given them this security. Even if the duty to support husband or wife, parents or children, was still established. (Though not brothers or sisters, not uncles or nephews, etc.)

In 1962 grain was distributed to needy families. Each labor group discussed how much should be set aside for this purpose. At that time there were those who had warned against this distribution, saying people would stop working if they could receive help. The brigade leadership was of the opinion that of course social aid must be given—security was important—but "the value of labor" must not be undermined. A whole little apparatus for social welfare then began to be built up.

Now social aid, as such, had been abolished. It was all being done in another way, a way which required neither applications, means-test, or check-ups. And the debate on the "negative effects of relief" was also entirely at an end. "Isn't it natural for people to work and do their best? After all, we aren't working for money. We're working for the revolution."

The average grain consumption was 215 kg. per person per year. Of this, 172 kg. consisted of a basic guarantee, paid out to everyone: old as well as young, whether working or not. This allocation was a citizen's right, and did not stand in any direct relation to how much work he or she did. Income from work was additional to this allocation.

This had meant that there were now only two households in Liu Ling Labor Brigade which were in a situation where they needed special help from the collective. This aid they received directly from the Revolutionary Committee under the "five guarantees." One could say that "social aid" had been abolished by making basic security the right of every citizen. But this reform had not been carried through without a great deal of political work. It was through political work that people's way of thinking had so changed that no one was even thinking in terms of such concepts as "aid" when it's a question of ensuring the old and the sick their daily grain requirements.

Li Hai-yuan said, "There's something wrong with my throat. I go to the doctor. He gives me injections and pills. Last year I was away from work for three months. My wife, too, is ill. She's quite past work. My income last year wasn't so big. But even though I was so ill for so long, I got as much grain as the others, and though she can't work any longer, my wife, too, got hers. This is new. It's very good. Previously, if one was ill, one got less than others, and special help. Now one gets as much as the others. There's nothing to discuss here. One doesn't have to ask for it. You just get it. It's very good."

At Liu Ling there has been no "free food" or collective dining halls. (Food is taken collectively to the harvesters up in the hills, and the students from town ate collectively in their dining hall—but that's another matter.) Nor is the new reform of the distribution system the same thing as "free food."

The cultural revolution has been a political revolution. It has meant deeper democracy. The poor and lower middle peasants exercise a broad democracy, where the decisions are all made at public meetings and general discussion implements economic policy and those reforms which are in the interest of the masses.

Those in China who followed Liu Shao-ch'i's line were talking about "efficiency" and the "low cultural level of the people" and the danger of undermining "the value of labor" and how useful piece-work was. And they were doing it in the name of socialism.

But when the poor and lower middle peasants at Liu Ling applied the deeper democracy they had fought for and obtained during the cultural revolution in order to carry out a reform of the distribution system to create absolute basic security for all citizens, they did not undermine "the value of labor" nor did they render the administration "inefficient."

For the principle of distribution required a new attitude to work. When people at Liu Ling talk about working for "the revolution, for the world revolution" this is no empty ceremonious phrase-making. Its real content, among other things, is that they are working so that Li Hai-yuan and his wife shall get their grain.

For in northern Shensi grain does not fall from heaven. Behind the grain of which Li Hai-yuan said, "You don't have to ask for it. You just get it. It's very good," lies a lot of hard work. Sweat and effort and thought, as he said in 1962 when speaking of agricultural work. And this is something no one in Liu Ling is ignorant of.

But it lay in the interests of the majority to strengthen the collective property. Only then could they have security. The simplified administration meant that the labor brigade was reinforced. A labor group is only a labor group. With this reinforcement of the brigades and the simplified administration it became possible to implement the new distribution system. Guaranteed security does not make people lazy—as so many bourgeois and revisionist experts had asserted it would—it makes work meaningful. The work is, and remains, hard, burdensome. But people are conscious of its significance, its necessity. They are working for the world revolution.

Polemical Digression

It may be interesting to see how these events are described in contemporary Soviet propaganda:

. . . In the Chinese countryside the poor peasants still constitute a large part of the population. Owing to illiteracy and the lack of objective information their political horizon is narrow. The extremely limited nature of the material needs of this part of the population who to a considerable extent get their livings by a redistribution of incomes within the cooperative (distribution by number of persons in each family, not by achievement) means that demands for a general leveling and reduction of consumption to the existing level of the poor peasants fall on fertile soil in this environment. . . . Precisely the poorest part of the rural population, which constitute the majority of the peasants, therefore at least offer no active resistance to Mao Tse-tung's policies. . . . As the Chinese newspapers witness, the struggle in the countryside is chiefly being fought out over concrete problems connected with the organization of production and living conditions. . . . Mao Tse-tung's policies arouse resistance among that part of the peasantry who, within the framework of the existing cooperatives, were able to improve their conditions and raise their standard of living during the short period of "regulation" (1961–65). Openly or covertly they protest against the neglect of material stimuli, against the general mania for leveling and the abrogation of income distribution by achievement. But this layer of the rural population has been frightened and terrified by the "cultural revolution" and as yet has not started an organized and active struggle to protect its interests . . . . The goal of the socialist society, *Lenin* stressed, is to secure "full well-being and free, all-round development for all its members." The Maoists have rejected this goal. . . . The leveling mania has thrust aside distribution by achievement, material stimulus has been replaced by non-economic compulsion.*

Not least curious in this curious Soviet text from 1969 is the quotation from Lenin. From the text it would seem as if this was some Leninist hope as to the goal of socialist society. A pretty and desirable Utopia. Had the anonymous Soviet theorist been more explicit about his sources, it would have transpired clearly that this is simply not the case. The Lenin quotation above is from the Russian Social Democratic Labor Party's discussion of its program in 1902. In Lenin's proposed program the sentence here quoted begins with the words:

The real emancipation of the working class requires a social revolution. . . .
—Lenin, *Collected Works*, VI, p. 28†

But not only is the social revolution necessary, it is a very specific revolution. The quote continues:

. . . i.e., the abolition of private ownership of the means of production, their conversion into public property, and the replacement of capitalist production of commodities by the socialist organization of the production

*From "The Situation in China and the Situation in the Communist Chinese Party at the Present Stage," in *What is Maoism?*, Novosty Press Agency, 1969. [Our translation—Ed.]
†V. I. Lenin, *Collected Works*, Vol. II: January 1902–August 1903 (Moscow, Foreign Languages Publishing House, 1961; issued by Lawrence & Wishart, London).

of articles by society as a whole, with the object of ensuring full well-being and free, all-round development for all its members.

The importance of this question lies in quite a different direction from that the Soviet commentator is pointing out. Plekhanov had suggested the following phrase:

> . . . and in the planned organization of the social production process so as to satisfy the needs of both society as a whole and its individual members . . .
>
> —Lenin, *Collected Works,* VI, p. 68

Lenin noted:

> Not accurate. *Such* "satisfaction" is "given" by capitalism as well, but *not to all* members of society and *not in equal degree.*
>
> —Lenin, *Collected Works,* VI, p. 68

And he wrote:

> Organization of that kind will, perhaps, be provided even by the trusts. It would be more definite to say "by society *as a whole*" (for this covers planning and indicates who is responsible for that planning), and not merely to satisfy the needs of its members, but with the object of ensuring *full* well-being and free *all-round* development for *all* the members of society.
>
> —Lenin, *Collected Works,* VI, p. 54

In reality here is the difference between Soviet revisionist ("provided even by the trusts") and Chinese Communist economic policies. The question of who are "responsible for that planning."

In China the effort to

> implement the teaching of Marx that only by emancipating all mankind can the proletariat achieve its own final emancipation
>
> —Mao Tse-tung, March 7, 1968, Directive

is a very conscious one.

58

The struggle between the two lines in Liu Ling has been a struggle about who are to be "responsible for that planning." The investments now being made have the conscious aim that through

> the socialist organization of the production of articles by society as a whole . . . create those material conditions, which alone can form the real basis of a higher society, a society in which the full and free development of every individual forms the ruling principle.
>
> — Marx, *Capital* I, esp. p. 592*

And to know what Lenin had to say on the subject of "working for the revolution," one should turn to Lenin himself, not to the Soviet quotation-hunters:

> . . . It is the beginning of a revolution that is more difficult, more tangible, more radical and more decisive than the overthrow of the bourgeoisie, for it is a victory over our own conservatism, indiscipline, petty-bourgeois egoism, a victory over the habits left as a heritage to the worker and peasant by accursed capitalism. Only when *this* victory is consolidated will the new social discipline, socialist discipline, be created; then and then only will communism become really invincible . . . Communism begins when the *rank-and-file* workers display an enthusiastic concern that is undaunted even by arduous toil to increase the productivity of labor, husband *every pood of grain, coal, iron* and other products, which do not accrue to the workers personally or to their "close" kith and kin, but to their "distant" kith and kin, i.e. society as a whole, to tens and hundreds of millions of people united first in one socialist state, and then in a union of Soviet republics . . . More concern about providing this pood of grain and pood of coal needed by the hungry workers and ragged and barefoot peasants *not* by *haggling*, not

*Karl Marx, *Capital*, trans. Moore and Aveling (New York, International Publishers, 1967).

59

in a capitalist manner, but by the conscious, voluntary, boundlessly heroic labor of plain workingmen . . . First show that you are capable of working without remuneration in the interests of society, in the interests of all the working people, show that you are capable of "working in a revolutionary way," that you are capable of raising productivity of labor, of organizing the work in an exemplary manner, and then hold out your hand for the honorable title "commune."

——Lenin, "A great beginning," July 1919, Collected Works, XXIX, pp. 411, 427, 428, 431*

Communist labor in the narrower and stricter sense of the term is labor performed gratis for the benefit of society, labor performed not as a definite duty, not for the purpose of obtaining a right to certain products, not according to previously established and legally fixed quotas, but voluntary labor, irrespective of quotas; it is labor performed because it has become a habit to work for the common good, and because of a conscious realization (that has become a habit) of the necessity of working for the common good—labor as the requirement of a healthy organism.

It must be clear to everybody that we, i.e., our society, our social system, are still a very long way from the application of this form of labor on a broad, really mass scale.

But the very fact that this question has been raised, and raised both by the whole of the advanced proletariat (the Communist Party and the trade unions) and by the state authorities, is a step in this direction.

To achieve big things we must start with little things.

——Lenin, "From the destruction of the old social system to the creation of the new," April 11, 1920, Collected Works, XXX, p. 517†

*V. I. Lenin, Collected Works, Vol. XXIX: March–August 1919 (Moscow, Progress Publishers, 1965; issued by Lawrence & Wishart, London).

†Ibid., Vol. XXX: September 1919–April 1920.

I have not quoted this just to show up the Soviet propagandists as liars. This can be done without benefit of such lengthy quotations. Nor to show that they are clearly taking sides in the class struggle (read carefully what they say on the one hand about the poor peasants "who constitute the majority of the peasantry" and, on the other, about their opponents in the villages of China); but because these people I am writing about—peasants deep in the interior of China—are now carrying through a social transformation of historic importance. Mao Tsetung is fulfilling the work of Lenin. This I simply state as a fact—anyone who so wishes can check it for himself, by reading Lenin.

Tung Yang-chen in World Politics

It has been raining for two days. Walking up the path by the stream we slip on the loess. During the night the water has cut its way into the cabbage field just above the village. Great chunks of earth have come tumbling down. The cabbages are hanging out over the ravine. The stream is heavy with silt and the Nan River is turbid. The fields are floating away in the rain, and the bare hills show deep gullies.

Tung Yang-chen hasn't changed much these last seven years. Others have. Feng Chang-yeh is grown much older, he looks worn and is so weary he drops off to sleep at the evening meeting, and has to be woken up by Tsao Chen-kuei. But Tung Yang-chen looks just the same. Reticent, morose. He has always been known as a hard worker. And still is.

In the morning before starting work on my interviews I'd been listening to my radio. The transistor is small and old, but Mau Pei-hsin had helped me to put up a big aerial. Now I'd been listening to Australia and the BBC and the Voice of America and Moscow. Up here in the hills reception is good.

And on the radio there has been talk about China, and there have been speculations and reports from Hong Kong, and on the BBC an expert on Chinese questions gave a lecture on Chinese politics. It all sounded very interesting. But was quite meaningless. Nothing but "high politics."

Real politics are decided by people like Tung Yang-chen. That he was morose and reticent, that he's never been very popular (but not particularly disliked, either) is neither here nor there. What has been crucial is that he has carried out a policy that has been necessary; he was chairman of the construction team.

"I participated in the criticism of the autumn of 1966. I wrote no big character posters. After all, I didn't know how to write. It was Mau Pei-hsin who had to do the writing. I criticized the party secretary, Feng, for not putting politics first. He had neglected politics. He was separating himself from the masses. He'd turned into an official and had been following the black line. He had neglected construction work. It was a contradiction among the people. He was no enemy. The masses helped Feng to criticize himself, and that was why he is still able to be a cadre.

"In the spring of 1967 we formed a construction team. Those who were capable of the heaviest work joined it. There were twenty-four of us. I was chosen work-leader. People thought I knew how to work. If people aren't satisfied with me, if they think I'm behaving in the wrong way or not working well, they can depose me. At any time. That's how things are here. And I don't get any extra pay for being work-leader. That never happens here.

"This is heavier work than what I used to do in the fields. But I'm not shy of work. I've worked all my life and I like it. It's as Chairman Mao says: we aren't afraid of hard work.

"We study Mao Tse-tung Thought. My job is to lead these studies in the labor group, and then apply them in practice. First the entire brigade discusses the problems on the basis of Mao Tse-tung Thought, and then decides what's to be done. My labor group, of course, can't make decisions about the over-all plan. That's something for everyone to decide. Nor can it be decided from above; it has to be decided from below. In our planning work we base our decisions on Chairman Mao. Well, that's how we began in the spring of 1967.

"The first task was to level the fields in the valley. They had to be surrounded with embankments to prevent erosion. The little fields had to be put together into larger ones, and the earth cleared of stones. We use water level instruments. The fields must be made quite flat. The embankments we make up from beaten earth. In this way the rainwater is retained. The soil doesn't dry out like it used to. That spring we finished 30 mu.

"In the autumn of 1967 and the spring of 1968 we dug three wells. Drought is a dangerous enemy. We had to fight the drought. The wells were 13 yards deep. And faced with stone. We had to cut the stone for them. Now they give us water all the year round. The brigade bought electric pumps from the cooperative at Yenan. They are made in China. With their motors they cost about 300 Y apiece. Each well can irrigate 20–30 mu of soil. Without irrigation we get 400 jin corn per mu. With irrigation we get 800 jin per mu.

"We terraced the slopes. Six terraces, twenty mu. The terracing stops the erosion. The rainwater is retained. The harvests become bigger. On the slopes the fields yield about 100 jin per mu. And the soil is washed away when it rains. After terracing, the fields give 300 jin per mu. And there is no erosion. Down in the valley where the soil is better the terracing makes the yield go up from 300 to 500 jin per mu.

"Last winter we dug three more big wells. Deep and faced with stone. They are irrigating 60 more mu. We are building erosion dams in the stream. We've already built ten such. Just now we are having to give a hand to get in the apple harvest. There are lots of apples this year. Afterward we shall begin in the valley over toward the village of Hutoma. Before the frost comes we must do all the embanking and leveling work.

"We'll be getting help from the youngsters. They're here to learn how to work. They've got to be re-educated. In our labor group Kao Yi-hsin is responsible for this. He's from Sian. He works well. He gives a hand with the planning. After all, he has been trained for this sort of work. He's a big help.

"Generally speaking these young people are good. It's a help for them to learn to work. Afterward, when the ground is frozen, we'll start working on the erosion dams up the gully. If we are to put an end to the worst erosion we need to build about ten more dams this winter."

Looking closely at world politics and world history you will always see a Tung Yang-chen carrying boulders. But what does it really mean when Tung Yang-chen now says that they start with Mao Tse-tung Thought study meetings when they are to plan the work?

To understand this in a correct fashion it is necessary to establish from where Liu Ling started to build. In *Report from a Chinese Village* the older peasants described the situation before Liberation. But one can take other—more general—descriptions.

They all agree: recurrent famines during which a large part of the population had to leave their home-counties and another part starved to death. Sharp class distinctions. The larger part of the population living in deep poverty. Underemployment and lack of working-force during harvests. Heavy erosion and soil destruction. Crushing taxation, usury and land rents. That was the situation.

Even after the parasitical classes had been smashed and land reform carried through the situation in Liu Ling was serious.

In Liu Ling—as all over China—they talk about the "struggle between the two lines." That is a correct description. In the Soviet Union and among the "Western" so-called "China-experts" it has been fashionable to speak of a struggle between the realists and the revolutionary

65

romantics. Mao Tse-tung is—according to this—a romantic. That is wrong.

The difference between what Liu Shao-ch'i said in 1951:

> In the socialization of agriculture, it is absolutely
> impossible for agriculture to attain collectivization
> without industrial expansion and without the realiza-
> tion of industrialization.

and what Mao Tse-tung said in 1955:

> "In agriculture, with conditions as they are in our
> country cooperation must precede the use of big
> machinery . . .

is not just a difference between 1951 and 1955 or between
shades of meanings. The difference is an expression of the
two different approaches to the question of how China
could develop.

On August 5, 1949 the State Department released the
text of a letter that had been sent from the Secretary of
State, Dean Acheson, to the President of the United States,
Harry S. Truman. In that letter Dean Acheson said:

> The population of China during the eighteenth and
> nineteenth centuries doubled, thereby creating an
> unbearable pressure on the land. The first problem
> which every Chinese government has had to face is that
> of feeding this population. So far none has succeeded.

Mao Tse-tung criticized the White Paper and Dean Acheson's letter. On September 16, 1949, he discussed the
question of overpopulation/revolution (a false question)
and then he wrote:

> According to Acheson, China has no way out at all.
> A population of 475 million constitutes an unbearable
> pressure and, revolution or no revolution, the case is
> hopeless. Acheson pins great hope on this; although he
> has not voiced this hope, it has been revealed by a
> number of American journalists—through the allega-

tion that the Communist Party of China will not be able to solve its economic problems — that China will remain in perpetual chaos and that her only way out is to live on United States flour, in other words, to become a United States colony.

And Mao Tse-tung asked:

Is it true that "so far none has succeeded"? In the old Liberated Areas in northwestern, northeastern, and eastern China, where the land problem has already been solved, does the problem of "feeding this population," as Acheson puts it, still exist? The United States has kept quite a number of spies or so-called observers in China. Why have they not ferreted out even this fact?

And Mao Tse-tung wrote — what now and then has been quoted to support the thesis that he is a "revolutionary romantic":

Of all things in the world, people are the most precious. Under the leadership of the Communist Party, as long as there are people, every kind of miracle can be performed. We are refuters of Acheson's counter-revolutionary theory. We believe that revolution can change everything, and that before long there will arise a new China with a big population and a great wealth of products, where life will be abundant and culture flourish. All pessimistic views are utterly groundless.

Now — twenty-one years later — it is very easy to see who was right and who was wrong, Acheson or Mao Tse-tung. (It would have been easier for the public in the United States and Sweden and other countries to see this if so many "experts" — among them people who knew better — for one reason or another, fear being one of them, had not misled the public so many times these twenty-one years.)

Whether one likes them or not, the facts are very

67

simple; China has no foreign debts. She has paid back everything she has borrowed or bought on credit since 1949 (including the Korean war debts to the Soviet Union). The currency is stable. Industry and technology are developing (including H-bombs and satellites). There is no famine. The standard of life is going up. These facts are not debatable. They have nothing to do with what Jan Myrdal likes or does not like, believes or does not believe or what the reader might or might not think about Jan Myrdal. They are just plain facts.

The conflict between the political lines of Liu Shao-ch'i and Mao Tse-tung first appeared as small differences in emphasis. But between this difference in emphasis a very real political conflict was hidden. Chen Po-ta said on October 4, 1955, in the Central Committee:

As Comrade Mao Tse-tung pointed out in his report, socialist industrialization is not something that can be carried out in isolation, separate from agricultural co-operation; our country must, therefore, adopt the policy of keeping agricultural cooperation in step with socialist industry. We cannot stand with one foot planted on socialist industry and the other on small-peasant economy. The victory of socialism is unthinkable unless we win over the five hundred million strong rural population to take part in socialist construction. The draft Decisions criticize the illusions harbored by certain comrades who are quite content with things as they are in the countryside, and with the small peasant economy. The Party must criticize such mistaken ideas. At the Third Conference on Mutual Aid and Cooperative Work called by the Central Committee in October 1953, Comrade Mao Tse-tung had this to say: "If positions in the countryside are not held by socialism, capitalism will assuredly occupy them. How then can we say that we will take neither the socialist nor the capitalist road?"

It is an invariable law that once the feudal land system is overthrown, a struggle begins in rural areas in which the choice lies between the capitalist or the socialist roads. It is either the one or the other: there is no middle course. Some comrades took quite a radical stand in their attitude towards the bourgeois-democratic revolution, but once they pass through that stage of the revolution, they remain quite content with the peasants having got back their land. So they loiter at the crossroads between socialism and capitalism, and are actually more interested in preserving the small-peasant economy than in giving a lead in its transformation to a socialist agriculture. Such comrades fail to realize that a small-peasant economy is not a paradise for the peasantry, but a garden in which capitalism grows. We have Lenin's dictum on this: "Small production engenders capitalism and the bourgeoisie continuously, daily, hourly, spontaneously, and on a mass scale."

It is impossible to compromise with a small-peasant economy. To entertain such an idea is mere self-deception.

I have quoted Chen Po-ta from this discussion because he supported the line of Mao Tse-tung. But also to show how the discussion was carried on in the Central Committee and that it was the line of Mao Tse-tung that in the main was victorious in the period from 1949 onward.

If the Liu Shao-ch'i line had been victorious then agricultural cooperation would have been put off while waiting for "the realization of industrialization."

Before such an industrialization could have been realized, a long time would have lapsed. The countryside would not have remained unchanged. The land reform would have become nothing more than the prelude of a new class-differentiation in the countryside. The Chinese revolution would have been another peasant revolution, like so many others. (An Asian Mexico.)

The erosion and soil destruction would have continued.

No capital would have been available to undertake the necessary—and costly—construction works to check them. Class differentiation in the countryside would have been rapid. Improved agricultural techniques (a "green revolution") would have increased the power of the rich peasants; forced the majority of small peasants down to the status of land-less seasonal workers.

Underemployment and capitalist agriculture would have meant that millions and millions of Chinese peasants would have been forced to the cities. There they would have formed ever-growing rings of deep slum around the towns. Areas inhabited by a "surplus" population.

Capital would have accumulated in a few hands. The majority of the rural population would remain on (or sink to) subsistence level. There would have been no basis for the development of light industries in the hinterlands. The newly rich peasants would, though, be a market for the luxury industries in the coastal cities.

The industrialization of China by means of her internal resources would have been impossible. China would have had to turn to the "super-powers" for "aid," investments; PL 480 farm surplus grain would have been supplied from the United States.

Note that I am not describing a fictional situation; I am describing India. The Liu Shao-ch'i line would have led China to the situation where India is today.

Liu Shao-ch'i often used words like "proletariat" and "Marxism-Leninism" and "socialism" but his line during the whole period was weighted in favor of a capitalist development in the countryside.

At certain times he gained influence. His ideas then reflected the needs of certain classes in China. When in 1961 Liu Shao-ch'i said:

> The free market must be maintained. The rural free market may produce some form of capitalism, some bourgeois elements, and some upstarts; and some small

traders and peddlers may become upstarts. . . . That some bourgeois elements appear in society is not frightening, for we are not afraid of the flooding of capitalism,

then he belonged to that group within the party of which Mao Tse-tung in 1955 had said that they:

usually take the standpoint of the bourgeoisie and the rich peasants or that of the well-to-do middle peasants who have a spontaneous tendency to take the capitalist road.

There was nothing "dreamy" or romantic about Mao Tse-tung's line. It accorded with the historical necessities: also with the needs of the vast majority. In the given situation (underemployment/labor shortage, soil destruction/poor harvests, peasant poverty/beginning class differentiation) one had to begin to solve problems by collective effort and organization before mechanization was possible. This has turned out to be correct. Liu Ling has raised its output, has overcome many difficulties.

But this line hasn't been embraced by "everyone." Liu Shao-ch'i was not an individual "everyone" objected to. He was expressing the political needs of certain definite groups. Again and again he suffered defeat. But he had a social base for his policy. The rich peasants, the bourgeoisie and the well-to-do middle peasants with their spontaneous tendency to take the capitalist road. Liu Shao-ch'i was their spokesman. He was powerful because the class struggle in China was not over. New privileged classes were striving for power in the countryside after the defeat of the landlords and inside the party itself the representatives of the old scholar-bureaucrats were once more emerging. Liu Shao-ch'i expressed their ideology when he spoke to the students in 1957 and said:

Work hard on the land for three to five years . . you have culture, but the peasants don't . . . When you maintain good relations with the peasants and possess three qualifications, you will be able to become a cadre at the hsiang, hsien, or provincial level; or you may reach the Party Central Committee, but that depends on your ability . . .

Liu Shao-ch'i saw the emergence of new privileged strata in the Soviet Union, but the interpretation he put on this was the one he told the students in 1952:

The Soviet Union is free of exploitation; one who dresses oneself smartly and wears jewels is one who labors well. Unless one labors well, one cannot possibly wear such smart dresses.

His view of life was that of a careerist. As in his oft-quoted words from 1960:

When you don't think of your personal benefit, you will achieve it. Take a small advantage and you will suffer a big disadvantage; but suffer a small disadvantage, and you will gain a big advantage.

The cultural revolution was not a struggle between Mao and Liu but between different classes and their representatives in China. The cultural revolution was a social struggle.

Tung Yang-chen had begun to learn to read during the cultural revolution. As in most families, the children have come home from school and tried to teach their parents to read. Tung Yang-chen learns reading in *Quotations from Chairman Mao Tse-tung*. And he reads:

The masses have boundless creative power. They can organize themselves and concentrate on places and branches of work where they can give full play to their energy; they can concentrate on production in breadth and depth and create more and more undertakings for their own well-being.

Tung Yang-chen says that this is correct. Thus one should

work. His daughter has taught him. Character by character they have studied, thought by thought. Now he says that Chairman Mao is quite right about all this.

One could say that Mao Tse-tung's line corresponds to the real conditions in the Chinese countryside. One can say that his line has the support of the poor peasants and the lower middle peasants; of the vast majority. They see this line as a means of building up the country. Experience has shown they are right. And Tung Yang-chen says that Mao Tse-tung is perfectly right.

But this isn't the whole story. It must also be borne in mind that Mao Tse-tung's line did not arise spontaneously in the villages. Tung Yang-chen has not formed these ideas by himself. On the contrary. He was extremely suspicious of cooperative agriculture.

"Most agreed to turn the labor group for mutual help into a farmers' cooperative; but I thought that as I had both animals and land, I ought to be able to manage on my own, and that if I was in want of labor, I could perfectly well hire people. So I said that I had no use for any sort of farmers' cooperative. I kept my independence and worked for myself on my own land."

That's what Tung Yang-chen had told me in 1962 about his first reaction to the cooperative agriculture of the fifties. Tung Yang-chen's father had been one of the martyrs of the revolution. Tung Yang-chen had been given some land during the land reform. Of his own accord, spontaneously, he had begun to think of hiring laborers.

What Tung Yang-chen said in 1962 is capable of more general expression: Peasant revolutions—frequent in China, as in other countries—can lead to the downfall of the landlords and the tax-gatherers, and to re-distribution of the land. But then the same old game starts all over again. No peasant revolution by itself is capable of creating a new social system.

Mao Tse-tung has never been a "peasant revolutionary" (as an earlier generation of "China experts" used to call him). So when one says that Mao Tse-tung's line corresponds to realities in the Chinese countryside and commands the support of the poor and lower middle peasants, one must also add that Mao Tse-tung Thought is leading the work at Liu Ling. And that is why politics comes first. For had there been no political discussions, Tung Yang-chen, of his own accord, would have striven to become a rich peasant with laborers, hired by the day, working for him.

The Chinese revolution is not a peasant revolution; but it is a revolution which has the support of the poor and lower middle peasants and which has been carried out in their interest.

Noodles, Pigs, and Revolution

At Liu Ling the old stable had been pulled down. Big new sheds for the animals had been built a hundred yards further to the south. Where the old stable used to stand, stone caves had been built for the new noodle factory, its workers and also for people who look after the animals.

Liu Ling is no particularly prosperous or model People's Commune. In other places the brigades are running whole industries. All Liu Ling Brigade has is its noodle factory. Though this is typical.

The raw materials come from the village's own agriculture: potatoes, beans, kaoliang, maize. But now these raw materials are worked up within the brigade and the noodles are sold as a finished product to the cooperative in town. The brigade's own households can buy noodles at a special price. Today Lo Han-hong is working in the noodle factory: "It was at our annual meeting in 1965 that I quit my job as brigade bookkeeper. The matter had been discussed. There was a lot for the bookkeeper to do. My training and education weren't up to it. I hadn't studied long enough. So I myself suggested that the brigade should elect Li Chi-chuan, who had been through Higher Middle School, instead. And so he was elected. As for me, the meeting sent me to work in the noodle factory. I was to learn this work. We had begun planning the noodle factory at the new year 1962–63. We wanted to develop the brigade's economy. Chairman Mao had recommended the establishment of light industries out among the brigades in the countryside. In 1965 we had come into contact with a knowledgeable old worker from Chichan, by name Li Kou-wan. I was one of those designated by the meeting to be his pupils.

"When I was sent to work in the noodle factory, I felt unsure. I knew nothing about such work. I was afraid of being a failure. But I read Chairman Mao and got the right attitude to the work. Now I understand the entire process here at the noodle factory. One learns as one works.

"Usually there are twelve of us at work here. At harvest time, when there's a shortage of labor, some of us go out and work in the fields. At other times, when less labor is needed for agriculture, we take in more here.

"It was difficult to begin with. Myself I was dubious whether noodle manufacture wouldn't prove too much for us. Technically, it isn't so simple as it seems. But we followed Chairman Mao's line and decided to have the courage to act.

"The noodle factory uses our own raw materials and gives the brigade extra income."

But the noodle factory at Liu Ling also had other functions. The new pig-sties had been built beside it. There Ma Hai-hsiu was feeding the factory waste to his breeding stock.

In this way the brigade had been able to supply its households with domestic pigs. Thus the household waste could be utilized better and the families' meat consumption increased—each household was now slaughtering and eating one fatted pig a year. The goal was for each household to breed up two domestic pigs a year. In this way the village would be able to contribute to the cities' meat supply and earn extra income for its families.

These domestic pigs, it should be pointed out, do not conflict with a collective economy. For as long as the households function individually—and that will still be for quite a while—the domestic pig is the most rational means of exploiting the individual households' waste.

In the collective economy these individual domestic pigs have an important function. The households deliver the manure to the labor group for vegetable cultivation —and receive work-points in payment. Noodle factory–domestic pigs–manure: all are part of a general development plan for the Liu Ling Brigade.

"In our labor group for vegetable cultivation," said its former chairman Ching Chung-ying, who is now retired and has the status of older experienced worker in the group, "in our vegetable growing group we have raised production during the cultural revolution. We have increased the yield from 7,000–8,000 jin per mu to 14,000 –15,000 jin per mu. This is a big change. We have made it by studying Chairman Mao. We've used Mao Tse-tung Thought in practice. Formerly one of the difficulties in the way of raising production was that the leading cadres did not really participate in production. They wanted to lead. So they didn't really discuss things thoroughly with those who did the work, nor did they listen to their advice. But today everyone who works discusses everything that has to do with production, puts forward many suggestions. Formerly, work-points governed the work. And distorted it. Now we're working for the revolution. The most important thing is not whether the work is individually profitable. We've dropped that system. The most important thing is whether our work is necessary to production.

"Today we use more fertilizer. That was something we discussed in detail. We've raised the quantity of animal manure from 4,000 jin per mu to 12,000–13,000 jin per mu. If we've been able to do this, it is because more manure has been available. We studied Chairman Mao. Out of our own resources we had to increase the available quantities

77

of animal manure. The masses discussed the matter most thoroughly, and we decided to increase the number of pigs in the brigade so that each household should breed up two.

"We also decided to arrange things in such a way that the brigade could supply all its households with piglets. We built sties for breeding-pigs, next to the noodle factory. That was how we increased the brigade's available manure.

"The labor group for vegetable cultivation credits each household work-points for its manure. A hundred jin yield one work-point. Formerly, before the cultural revolution, the households often used to retain their own human excrement for their own private plots of ground. We don't do that any longer. During the cultural revolution our political awareness has increased, and the masses have realized we are working for the revolution. Now the households give their human excrement to the vegetable team for compost. And get work-points for it. That's how we're able to increase output. And now the masses realize that collective work yields better results."

As vegetable output has risen at Liu Ling, it has been possible to reduce the private plots of land. The question is currently being discussed—though it is not yet decided—whether private plots should not be suppressed altogether. Hitherto though, they have supplied families with their vegetables.

Ma Hai-hsiu said, "I don't feel too well. My stomach isn't well. It wasn't well last time you were here. And it still isn't well. These years haven't been too bad. In 1963 we had quite a decent harvest. The weather hasn't been too bad any of these years. I went on working in the labor group for vegetable cultivation up to September, 1968. Then I went over to looking after the pigs.

"Chairman Mao had said there must be a rise in pig-breeding. So, in 1966 we started work on the brigade pig-sty. Our goal was to produce so many piglets that every member of the brigade could have one pig. That would mean much more manure. Now we have eleven sows and three boars. Members of the brigade can buy piglets from the brigade and breed them up.

"I'm responsible for the pig-sty. I get help with the heavy part of the work from the noodle factory. There's a lad from Peking who's working there. He helps me. His name is Tian Yuan-chao. He carries water and clears out the dung. It's too heavy work for me nowadays. In return, I lend them a hand with the lighter work in the noodle factory.

"Tian Yuan-chao's a good boy. He works very hard. He has come here to be re-educated by us poor peasants and lower middle peasants. While we've been working together, I've told him about my life and experiences. He says he'd never forget it. After all, he says, he's grown up in the new society; so its very important for him to realize what hard lives we've had to lead. He wanted to be re-educated by us old people, who've had experience. The youngsters from the town are good. They're learning how to work now, and understand why we must follow the socialist way and not the capitalist. They are also very respectful toward us old peasants.

"The whole question of pig-breeding was raised during the revolution. How can agriculture be developed? Agriculture needs more manure. How can we get more manure? That's the way we discussed things. And that's why we decided to breed more pigs. For pigs give good manure. We did all this in line with Mao Tse-tung Thought.

"I'm old, and I can't read. But we've studied Chairman Mao and I'm sure my memory doesn't fail me when I say that Chairman Mao has said that each pig is a small fertilizer factory. By raising the number of pigs we get more manure, and with more manure we can increase agricultural output. The whole discussion on pig-breeding grew out of the Mao Tse-tung Thought. We must stand on our own feet."

How Work is to be Evaluated

After long discussion the Liu Ling Brigade has changed over, this year, to a new method of calculating income from work.

The labor brigade is the smallest economic unit in Liu Ling. So distribution of income has to be based on its total earnings, i.e., not on the income of the labor groups. Labor groups are labor groups, nothing more.

Formerly each item of work, each task, had been attributed a certain value. So or so many work days' pay for each job. During the years 1963–65 this system had tended to develop into piece-work.

It had led to certain tasks being individually profitable, others less so. Those who managed the work were also in a position—by distributing the work—to affect the incomes of individual members of the brigade.

"During those years," said Mau Ke-yeh, "I felt it was a danger. As Liu Shao-ch'i's black line was followed, many loyal people suffered. Opportunists were able to make money for themselves. Those who were working for the collective, who saved and cared for the collective property, often came off badly. They were given low incomes, while egotistic people were getting high ones, even though it harmed the common cause. The opportunists were distorting our planning. They wanted to invest in short-term and profitable projects. And that wasn't good.

"What happened was that work came to be evaluated by a small group of leading cadres, who also distributed the work. And that was bad. As there was a bonus paid when the planned production was exceeded, people were enticed to lower the planned goals for production. Finally we reached a situation when the planned production was 100 jin per mu. As this was always exceeded, the bonus always had to be paid out and one always got extra incomes. This caused a heavy damage to our economy. It undermined our economy. The investments were made according to the planned production. Thus certain people could get out money for themselves that in reality ought to have gone to absolutely necessary investments.

"This was unfair. Even though everybody worked, some people got higher incomes and some were getting ever less. Everybody worked for himself."

That is what Mau Ke-yeh says late autumn 1969. But his description of himself as being worried about this is no rationalization in retrospect. When he was talking about the discussion at the beginning of the cultural revolution in the autumn of 1966, Li Hai-tsai said: "Mau Ke-yeh was very active from the outset. He talked a lot with the Red Guards and received many of them in his own home. After all, he was an old cadre, who had been working for the revolution for more than thirty years. But he was also chairman of the Liu Ling Labor Bridage's supervisory committee. Hearing this, the Red Guards got up and criticized Mau Ke-yeh at the meeting. After all, he was responsible. As chairman of the audit committee he should have intervened. When the Red Guards had spoken, the masses agreed with them. They criticized Mau Ke-yeh for failing to criticize the work of the cadres.

"Mau Ke-yeh made self-criticism to the masses. But from his self-criticism it also transpired that he had in fact raised these issues and criticized the cadres. But the cadres had been so poisoned by Liu Shao-ch'i's line that not only had they not listened to him, they had suppressed his criticisms. But he criticized himself for not having turned to the masses when his criticism had been silenced. Such was the content of Mau Ke-yeh's self-criticism in December, 1966.

"After the masses had heard him, they looked into the question and found he was right. He had criticized the cadres; but his criticisms had been silenced. So the masses accepted his self-criticism as honest, and agreed that he had been following the revolutionary line of Chairman Mao."

The basis of the new system of income distribution, introduced now, was that all members, whether working or not, should enjoy basic security in the form of grain. Income from work was additional to this basic security.

After these discussions, however, all forms of piece-work were abolished. Therefore no accounts were kept of what work had been done by whom or of individual performance. Only daily work-attendance was recorded. This meant that whether one was chosen to do this job or that job made no difference to one's income. Whether one dug or harvested, fetched manure from town or worked at the noodle factory, the day's work had the same value.

This also made it possible to do away with most book-keeping work—thus releasing more labor for production.

But, of course, people work differently. And attitudes to work vary. One person's working day is not the same as another's. This had to be taken into account.

Thus everyone's individual working capacity was evaluated at the annual meeting. This evaluation took into account not merely physical strength, but also other factors: their experience, thriftiness with the collective property, political awareness. The evaluation was not made by any committee or group of experts. At the annual meeting each person got up and said what he thought his own day's work was worth: 7 work-points, 9 work-points. After which

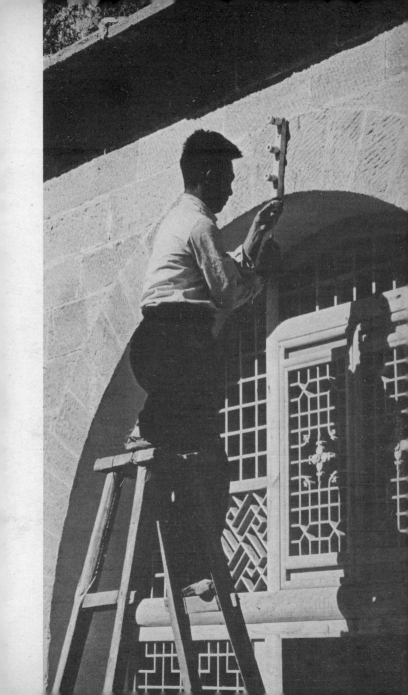

the meeting discussed the accuracy of this assessment and then decided what that member's day's work was in fact to be worth.

Under this system an old man like Ma Hai-hsiu could be allocated a considerably greater number of work-points for his work in the pig-sties than if only his physical strength or the actual job he was doing were taken into account. For now his general experience was added in: the advice he gave during discussions; his political work; the fact that he was taking charge of youngsters from Peking and taught them to work and in a good and understanding way gave them the right attitude to life and work.

Adult men normally get 7–9 work-points per day's work. Women get 6–7 points. This difference between the sexes is due to the stated fact that a woman's working day in production is shorter than a man's. Part of her time goes to household work. And this household work is individual in character, and receives no wage from the collective. The more the housework can be simplified by collective means (e.g. the mill), the closer the men's and the women's working day will approximate each other, and so also their work-points per working day. The difference between men and women is based on the different amount of time they put in at work. Not all women have households to look after; not all men are full-time workers. So there are women who get 9 points and men who get 6.

An unforseen difficulty had arisen during threshing. To get the threshing done in the shortest possible time, work went on at the threshing machine all round the clock. The annual meeting had made a decision that, in principle, no one should earn more than one day's pay a day: this, to prevent the piece-work system creeping in again by the back door. At the same time it was regarded as self-evident that those people who worked overtime during the nights at the threshing machine ought to receive some sort of compensation. So a record was kept of those who had worked nights, and the question was going to be taken up at the coming annual meeting. It was assumed that the meeting would allot them some extra days' pay.

But if this system of income distribution was to be carried through in practice, it was vital that the members should be conscious that they were working for the common good. Only when they put politics first could work be remunerated in this way.

The prevailing opinion in Liu Ling was that the system had shown itself capable of working. It simply wasn't true, as Liu Shao-ch'i had maintained, that each man has to work for himself. People didn't grow "lazier" just because no one was measuring how much they'd done, hour by hour. No one stayed away from the heavy construction work just because he could "earn as much" by pushing a dung-cart. Those who had uttered warnings against people's "innate laziness and egoism" had been proved wrong. The twenty-year-olds did not think old Ma Hai-hsiu should not get a proper income just because he had a pain in his stomach and hadn't the strength to carry buckets of water or clear out the dung.

"Ma Hai-hsiu is a man of great experience. He knows a great deal and offers much good advice."

In September, 1966, Came the Red Guards

Fu Hai-tsao:

"It was in the autumn of 1966 that the Red Guards came here. First, seven of them. The second time, ten. From September to December, 1966, various Red Guards came here. Each group stayed for a week or ten days. That was how the cultural revolution began among us.

"The Red Guards came with the book of quotations. They read out to us quotations we'd never heard before. They made speeches and arranged discussions. We welcomed them by beating on drums. They came to us in our caves. We warmed the kang for them, so they shouldn't catch cold. They paid their way. All of them.

"In the village there were some people who were afraid the Red Guards would cause trouble. My mother thought so. 'I don't understand a thing,' she said. But she's very old. She's over seventy. But the Red Guards were very polite to her. They called her 'Old Granny.' They were always very respectful to her. And so she changed her mind.

"The Red Guards were well organized. They divided themselves up and visited every household in the village. They read quotations and told us about the cultural revolution in Peking and Shanghai. Never before had we had so many strangers in the village. They asked us about our lives. They wanted to learn from us. They asked us how we were managing things here in the brigade. They entered into discussions with the leading cadres of the brigade and, at open meetings, asked about work-points and so forth.

"I got the book of quotations from them. They distributed it to various households. In the end we all had it. Those Red Guards meant a lot to us. And we went on reading the quotations after they'd gone. We read, and compared the quotations with what was being done here at Liu Ling, and came to the conclusion that a lot of things needed changing. Those who couldn't read the quotations themselves had them read to them aloud."

Ching Chung-ying:

"I had eight of them living in my home. They all came from Sian. They were about eighteen years old. They spread Mao Tse-tung Thought. They asked whether we had any problems in the brigade, whether the cadres had been making any mistakes. They mobilized the masses and held big discussions. They urged us to speak out openly and write big character posters. 'You must pluck up courage and criticize things that are wrong,' they told me. 'We are Chairman Mao's Red Guards. Chairman Mao supports the poor peasants. We aren't afraid of criticizing.'

"The Red Guards wanted to hear everything about how we used to live in the old society. I told them all about my life. I also told them how we'd had to sell my two youngest brothers during the 1928 famine. All this I told them as we sat in my cave. They were most sympathetic and said they would never forget the sufferings we poor peasants had had to go through.

"But, by telling them about this, I found Fifth Brother again—the one whom we sold for twenty-eight silver dollars. For the Red Guards afterwards went from Liu Ling to Lanchien. There they met a man called Mau Ying. When they told him about me, he said that he knew who my brother was, who had been sold for twenty-eight silver dollars. He lived in Shansi. So he wrote to Fifth

Brother and told him the whole story, and wrote to him that I was now living at Liu Ling. After that Fifth Brother wrote to me; and so, after all these years, we found each other again, thanks to the Red Guards. But so far no one has been able to tell me what happened to Fourth Brother."

Li Hai-tsai:

"We formed a reception committee in the brigade, to receive the Red Guards. They came marching in their hundreds of thousands towards Yenan, to learn the Yenan spirit. They came to learn and to spread the fire of the revolution. They came here too. And now it was a question of seeing to it they had a roof over their heads. They paid their way. Everything was done in an organized, orderly manner. We helped them to meet heroes of the revolution and old cadres. They often talked to Mau Ke-yeh, who had been in the revolution so long. It was from that time the cultural revolution began among us in earnest. For the Red Guards from Peking also talked with our youngsters in the village and formed a Red Guard section and began to criticize our cadres. That's something they'd never have dared to do before they met the Red Guards from the big cities."

The Health Insurance Reform

On January 13, 1969, the health insurance fund of Liu Ling Labor Brigade was formed. It is not called health insurance, however, but cooperative medicine. But, it is a health insurance scheme. After quite a lot of discussion, agreement was reached as to its mode of operation, and a board consisting of eight people was elected. The health insurance applies to all the 709 inhabitants of the labor brigade.

Today, all over China, the health insurance reform is being introduced in brigade after brigade. All of which may seem quite simple and self-evident. There's nothing very sensational about health insurance. But in point of fact the introduction of health insurance is one of the great, one of the truly sensational events in the China of the cultural revolution.

Formerly, the state employees, officials, industrial workers, and teachers had been assured medical care by the State. With the development of agricultural cooperatives and, later, as a result of the reform of the People's Communes, all of China's many hundreds of millions have been able to create basic security for themselves in matters of health. Today the health insurance reform has begun to be introduced all over China. There are variations between the different people's communes, but at Liu Ling the reform means that all members are assured of the free services of a doctor and free medicine within the brigade. If necessary, patients are remitted to the nearest hospital. There the health insurance fund pays all their costs up to 30 Y. Which is the equivalent of three weeks in hospital. If they have to stay longer in hospital and it costs more than 30 Y, then the brigade comes to their support, under the five guarantees.

When the health insurance fund was established, the brigade contributed a basic sum of 2,000 Y. The brigade also pays all the salaries of its own medical personnel. Members pay 1.50 Y a year. Schoolchildren and others make a further contribution by collecting medicinal herbs. The State's sale prices for medicines of various sorts have been reduced during the autumn of 1969 (penicillin in ampules of units of 200,000 has been reduced by 46 per cent; sulfathiazole tablets by 13.3 per cent; the average cut in prices has been 37 per cent). This drop in prices has been a direct and explicit part of the attempts to improve the general level of health and to facilitate the work of the health insurance funds.

This health insurance reform at Liu Ling was carried out after a discussion. Yang Kou-shen was one of those who had been of the opinion that, though in itself good, the reform was also dangerous: "Too many people will come asking for medicines. We'll lose the entire fund. We won't be able to manage it. Even if free medicine is a good idea, it's better that people should have to pay for their own medicines."

Only after several meetings was Yang Kou-shen convinced. Finally, after all these discussions, it was unanimously agreed, on January 13, 1969, to establish the fund.

"It had been toward the end of 1968 we had heard of cooperative medicine," said Wang You-nan, the brigade doctor and health officer. "We were opposed to Liu Shao-ch'i's black line. It was a soft knife. It killed people unawares. For there were doctors in the cities and it was there too—though most people live in the countryside—the good medical facilities existed. It was a medical service for the few. While the majority just had to suffer. It was difficult to go to town to see a doctor. You had to wait in line, and weren't treated well. It was all as Chairman Mao said: the Ministry of Health had become a ministry for urban overlords. In our discussions we agreed that the health policy in the country had been wrong.

"Everyone agreed about that. In our discussions we proceeded from the words of Chairman Mao: 'In medical and health work, put the stress on the rural areas.' We also took as our starting point Chairman Mao's observation that preventive medicine and the fight against the commonest diseases which affect large parts of the population are very important.

"It didn't take long until most people not only were in agreement about this, but also about cooperative medicine. But there were a few who were unsure. Some, of course, said it would be expensive; that we wouldn't be able to afford it. Others thought the State should pay both for medicine and health care.

"But together we studied Chairman Mao and followed Mao Tse-tung's teaching: fight self, criticize revisionism; and by and by Yang Kou-shen realized he'd been wrong. It was correct that medicine should be provided free. Starting with Chairman Mao, we talked things over until we were agreed it was no good our relying on the State. We must rely on ourselves. Where, anyway, was the State to get all that money from? If we asked the State for money instead of forming our own health insurance fund, it would simply mean we were undermining the national economy. That was not the right way to go about things, was it? That would be Liu Shao-ch'i's black line. All these conclusions we reached by studying Chairman Mao. Our discussions led to complete unanimity.

"Our commonest ailments here are rheumatism and influenza. I treat rheumatism by 'water acupuncture.' I make an injection of B_{12} at the acupuncture points. It's a new technique."

(Wang You-nan speaks of acupuncture. This calls for an explanation. Acupuncture is neither charlatanism nor is it superstition. It's an ancient Chinese method of treatment. A fine needle is inserted at certain points in the body. Nowadays the needles are sterilized each time. The method is much used in China, and is an efficient treatment in a number of cases—as I know, having myself opted for an acupuncture doctor on certain occasions when I've been ill in China.

At present the scientific basis for the effectiveness of the treatment is being studied. Like so much else in medicine it is a form of treatment which has developed empirically, and its theoretical grounds are still being clarified. Probably it affects both the lymphs and the vegetative nervous system.

Acupuncture is one of a number of methods. It is not "the" method. It is not used on all sorts of illness. Chiefly, it is applied against rheumatism, painful conditions of various sorts, illnesses caused by stress, stomach ulcers, etc. It is also used successfully against various sorts of deafness and blindness. Acupuncture is also alleged to strengthen the body's automatic defense mechanisms against inflammations. Acupuncture is not used against illnesses caused by parasites or T.B. or suchlike. The question is not: Acupuncture *or* "Western medicine." There is no conflict between those Chinese researchers who are studying acupuncture's mode of operation and those who have synthesized insulin.)

"The children are vaccinated twice a year. Most important of all is preventive medicine. Here in the brigade we carry out four health campaigns a year. We check up on the latrines and drinking water. In each labor group one person is responsible for sanitation and health, and also gives regular courses in hygiene, medicine and first aid. These persons who are responsible for

112

health hold a regular fortnightly meeting. At these meetings we study acupuncture, the symptoms of various illnesses and so forth. It is important that all healthworkers learn to recognize the symptoms of the serious diseases. These must be identified at the earliest possible moment.

"In spring and autumn we get quite a few infectious diseases. At present we've a number of cases of inflammation of the upper respiratory tract. At this time of year we get five or six patients coming to us every day. Winter and summer not so many. When I'm not receiving my patients, I work in the fields. I get paid just as much by the labor brigade for my day's work, whether I'm plowing or receiving patients."

Wang You-nan had begun to study medicine on his own. He had had no formal higher education. Wang Younan comes from Wangchiakou. In the winters of 1945 and 1946 he went to school at Liu Ling. He joined the army in 1947, when Hu Tsung-nan attacked Yenan. Was in many battles. Commanded a platoon. In 1951 he was demobilized from the People's Liberation Army and went back to agricultural work. In 1953 he was elected leader of a labor exchange group and was appointed herdsman in the East Shines Red Higher Agricultural Cooperative.

He had always been fond of reading and had become interested in health care and acupuncture. He had bought a couple of books about it in the bookshop at Yenan when he was in town. He had also bought a couple of needles and experimented on himself. In 1955 his friend Ma Juei-ching, the son of Ma Chen-hai, got pains in his stomach. He felt very ill. So he said to Wang Younan, "You can do something about it, can't you?"

After the treatment, Ma Juei-ching became well again, and thereafter Wang You-nan began curing minor aches and pains with acupuncture. And all the time he went on studying medicine, and buying new books. But the management of the work brigade paid no attention to him. Nor did they support him.

It was after the cultural revolution that the masses decided that he should be sent on study courses. By now he has attended several, both in the People's Commune and in town.

"First we discuss politics. Politics comes first. In medicine the chief question is: Whom do we serve? Then we study various methods of treatment. We learn hygiene, health care and pharmacology. We have also made a close study of diagnostics; all serious illnesses have to be remitted to the hospital in town. All heart cases, stomach ulcers, and such cases as may be cancer are sent to town. The courses are led by doctors from the city and from the province. The leader of the latest course in town has been Doctor Sung. He spoke on methods of treating rheumatism and instructed us in water-acupuncture. The method has been newly discovered, and according to Doctor Sung has proved most effective.

"Old Doctor Kao left the brigade in 1965. He had grown very old. Toward the end he was completely deaf and his sight was going. And that was why the health-care station, here in the brigade, came to an end.

"It is very important that health care shall be developed in the brigades and labor groups. Take Wang Fu-ying, at Wangchiakou, for example. He was suffering from pains in the small of his back. They tormented him, and in 1967 and 1968 he visited a doctor in town. Altogether he lost thirty working days waiting in line for the doctor in town. Besides losing income from work he had to pay out altogether 200 Y for treatment and his medicines. Now we have treated him. After three acupuncture treatments he feels well and has no pains. And if he needs help he comes to us. He no longer has to lose one or more working days getting into town and waiting his turn at the doctor's. And the medicine costs him nothing."

114

A New Sort of Intellectual

There are two traditional definitions of the word "intellectual." The one is "someone who has a higher education" and the other is "a person who devotes himself to scientific or literary activities."

But Wang You-nan had been a herdsman. Now he was a health worker and was training himself to become a doctor. This is a third sort of intellectual. For Wang You-nan is no anomaly. Let us take the brigade veterinary, and its midwife.

In 1962 it was said of Chang Chung-liang—at that time bookkeeper in the Liu Ling Labor Group—and his wife Chi Mei-ying: "He's nothing special. On the whole he's an honest fellow. He isn't very strong. He does not like talking with people. He is by nature uncommunicative and something of a recluse. But he is decent and honest. He has always had the reputation of being prudent and considerate. His wife, Chi Mei-ying, is a member of the Youth League. She jokes a lot and chatters all day long. Some years ago she attended a course and learned the new scientific methods of delivering babies. Latterly she has been midwife and attended most of the births in the village. Because of her, most children now survive. She is very well liked. Theirs is a happy marriage."

Now Chang Chung-liang says, "Work in the brigade is increasing all the time. We get more and more animals. According to Chairman Mao we ought to develop our animal-breeding still further. It is also important to agriculture. Animals provide manure.

"But animals also need looking after. And it's important that they're properly looked after. It's important to prevent diseases. If the animals fall sick, one has to know how to help them. In 1967 it became possible to train people to do this here in our district. And the brigade chose me.

"I'd had a little training before. When I was bookkeeper I used to study on my own, and in this way had raised my cultural level so that I could benefit by education. And then—I like animals.

"Each brigade was to send one person to study animal diseases. There are regular courses twice a year. So far I've attended six such courses. We learn, step by step. We learn how to prevent diseases among animals. We study various problems connected with looking after animals. We study animal diseases and how to cure them. Now I give medicines and injections and even minor treatment. As yet I have not learned how to operate. But we're still following our studies at these courses.

"Now the brigade is building sheds for its animals. I have to have my say in how they are planned, and see to it that they're built in such a way that the animals can keep warm in winter. Otherwise they'll get ill. It's also my business to see to it they're built hygienically and are easy to keep clean. I also have to keep an eye on the way the domestic pigs are treated. I'm responsible for all the animals.

"Animal diseases vary, just as human diseases do. Pneumonia and tuberculosis, for example. They can be treated. These last six days I've been combating parasites. They have to be watched all the time. They must be exterminated. I've given the animals pills and examined both the brigade animals and the domestic pigs. The households pay nothing for this.

"If the animals get seriously sick, then I must decide whether they can be cured or will have to be slaughtered. I do this in company with a more highly trained veterinary from the city. In the same way I have to decide whether people shall be allowed to eat the meat of animals which have had to be slaughtered, or whether it must be destroyed. All this is my responsibility.

"I get the same work-points for this veterinary work as I used to get for working in agriculture. Last year I got 2,800 work-points. Then I was away for a while. My mother is very old now. I asked for leave of absence to go and see her. In such cases we're always granted leave. Obviously.

"There are those who call looking after sick animals dirty work. But Chairman Mao has taught us not to be afraid of filth and excrement. And that's right. Chairman Mao has pointed out how necessary it is to develop stock-breeding. And that's why we are getting ourselves more and more animals, and why I'm studying all the time."

His wife, Chi Mei-ying, is still the brigade's midwife. She has been, ever since she went through her first course in 1958. "We've been successful in our work. Now the new-born babies don't die any more. Formerly 60 per cent of all new-born infants died. The old way of giving birth to children was unhygienic. Dangerous, both for mother and child. To begin with, it was necessary to spread a great deal of information. But now there are no more problems over childbirths. Now the women understand why hygiene is important. Today I deliver all the women in the village.

"I'm also responsible for infant care. I teach the women. It's cleanliness that's so important. Their clothes must be clean, their hands must be clean, their food must be clean. Cleanliness is the answer to disease. It is thanks to cleanliness our babies are surviving.

"Now the women, too, understand. At least, most women understand that three or four years should go by between pregnancies. Pregnancies that are too close together are damaging to health. Formerly many women were always pregnant. Most now understand that this is bad.

"But we must go on spreading information. There used to be some men who spoke against contraceptives. It was easier to convince the women. But now even none of the men are against them. Now everyone says they agree. But some families are thoughtless. And of course there are accidents too. I have to speak to them. It's the women's health that's in question, too. Today condoms are much cheaper than they were seven years ago. Now they cost only 1 Y per hundred. And no one is so poor he can't afford that.

"Other things are more problematic. There are so many bad old customs which must be combated. There are people who don't wash their clothes often enough. There are those who aren't careful enough about their food. Not everyone looks after their latrines properly. A latrine must be kept clean and free of smells. Dry earth must be used for covering them. There must be no flies. We have got quite a long way with our hygienic work, but not the whole way. That is why unremitting propaganda is needed against the old bad habits. Not to look after latrines properly, that's one such bad habit. Hygiene is a political question. So we must put in more work to get all the latrines clean and free of smells. The bad old habits are deep-rooted, but we're fighting them all the time, and things are getting better every year that goes by. This work we do during study meetings. To study and apply Mao Tse-tung Thought is a good method. Good things can be praised. During these studies many people have come to realize that latrines, too, are a political question. In this way they have in a living way studied Mao Tse-tung Thought and undergone a change of attitude."

It may not seem sensational, perhaps, that the farmers in a brigade in northern Shensi should have set up a health insurance fund or that they should be going to courses and educating themselves and taking responsibility for childbirths and carrying out hygiene campaigns and fighting the bad old habits and saying that latrines are a question of politics.

But in reality it's a sensation. The face of a revolution.

The Great Criticism at Liu Ling

The Soviet press, especially, has written that the cultural revolution was "directed against the party." Oddly enough, the Soviet indignation has been shared by the press of capitalist countries. Western writers have discovered that they can combine their dislike of Communism with a willingness to come to the aid of Communists who have reached "decision-making level." Remarkable though this may appear, there is nothing remarkable about it.

It was the leading Party members who were criticized at Liu Ling. In other places it was the leading Party members who were dismissed. But it has been Communists who started the cultural revolution and who have carried it through in the name of Communism.

When one speaks with Chinese Party members about this, they refer to Mao Tse-tung:

> All our cadres, whatever their rank, are servants of the people, and whatever we do is to serve the people. How then can we be reluctant to discard any of our bad traits?

The question facing such Communists as Mau Pei-hsin, who initiated the cultural revolution's great criticism of Liu Ling, was not whether this criticism was "directed against the Party" but whether the Party—contrary to what Marx and Engels have said in the Manifesto—can have any interests other than those of the proletariat. If leading groups within the Party had begun to establish interests of their own, had become "decision-makers" and were beginning to acquire privileges, then they no longer represented the Party. They were only its rubber stamp. And this, too, explains why the capitalist press was able to regard these wielders of power as "sensible Communists," feel solidarity with them, and write reports about anarchy and civil war and the collapse of China, as they did during the cultural revolution, when these wielders of power were being criticized by the people.

At Liu Ling the cultural revolution had been prepared by discussions and studies. The Red Guards had come to the village. Bringing with them the words of Mao Tse-tung, they had exhorted people to seriously criticize what was going on.

Mau Pei-hsin:

"Well, the first time I ever met the Red Guards I didn't really understand them. I wondered what they'd come here for. I wondered what business they had to be here. But I talked to them. We discussed the matter. And then I understood that they had come here as the voice of Chairman Mao and the Central Committee.

"Until the Red Guards arrived I hadn't read the quotations. I'd only heard about the works of Chairman Mao. But they were hard to get hold of. They were expensive too. Nor were they all that easy to read. That was why it was so important to me to get hold of the Quotations from Chairman Mao Tse-tung. I studied it closely. After I'd read it, I plucked up courage and wrote my first big character poster. And stuck it up outside on the wall.

"In it I criticized Feng and Tsao. They had not been following the revolutionary line of Chairman Mao. They hadn't given priority to grain output. They had neglected agriculture and become obsessed with quick returns.

121

"A lot of people came here to look at that big character poster. They came from the whole brigade and read it out loud to each other and began discussing matters. Until then there had not been any concrete criticism.

"And of course we had problems, here in the brigade. We spoke of learning from Tachai and we had sent Feng to Tachai to learn; but the result had been nothing but a lot of words. Nothing got done. I'd pondered this. So had many people. But we had said nothing out loud. Not until the Red Guards arrived and told us how they had stuck up big character posters in Peking and how they had criticized those in power for entering the wrong paths, did I pluck up courage and myself write a big character poster about how things were here in Liu Ling.

"From September 1966 on, many mass meetings were held. At them we discussed matters. We condemned Liu Shao-ch'i's revisionist line. We called him the Khruschev of China. We knew who that was. The Red Guards told me all about Liu. We talked about him among ourselves, by name. He was a powerful man. But we followed Mao Tse-tung's line and were not afraid of those in power. The emperor can be thrown off his horse. That's why I dared to criticize Liu Shao-ch'i.

"Liu Shao-ch'i's revisionist line was leading to the restoration of capitalism in the countryside. I spoke up at the meetings and pointed out that Liu Shao-ch'i regarded the countryside as backward; that he was neglecting agriculture; and that this was why the yield was growing too slowly. I should add that Liu Shao-ch'i regarded the cultural level of the countryside as so low, and its technology as so backward, that the masses were incapable of mechanization. In his view, everything would have to be postponed. We would have to proceed slowly. According to him we were so benighted, and our cultural level so low, all we could do was wait.

"I'm a Communist and it was the Party which told me

to return to the country to work on the mechanization of agriculture. I didn't agree with Liu Shao-ch'i. His attitude was revisionist and counter-revolutionary.

"We Party members studied the sixteen points from the meeting of the Central Committee. And it was in that spirit we now mobilized the masses and got them to openly express their criticisms. During these dicussions and mass meetings the cadres began to realize that they had been following the wrong line in their work.

"But our cadres weren't criminals. It was Liu who had been the criminal. Our cadres had merely been following his line. By these discussions the masses helped the cadres to gain insight into their own errors.

"This discussion went on for a whole year. We discussed how we could best make a real effort to raise production and advance the revolution. We made many practical improvements. We also discussed the various cadres' problems. We wanted to help them.

"In this way we began work with the construction team. We decided to make various improvements in the agricultural work. I was commissioned to look over the electrical system and improve maintenance at our machine park.

"In September-October, 1967, we'd got so far that we could agree in principle to change the management. It was to be simplified and unified. Then we discussed various cadres. Who should be changed, who should no longer hold leading positions. This was not done at mass meetings, but in groups within the various labor groups. After all, these were important questions. Any fool can get up and say he's following Chairman Mao's line. But that's not enough. It has to be discussed in detail. In this way we helped the cadres.

"By the summer of 1968 all this was more or less over. Party Secretary Feng had been following Liu Shao-ch'i's line, but with the help of the masses he had seen the error

123

of his ways and shown a genuine desire to change and said he was determined to follow the revolutionary line. And that was why the masses decided that he should remain a leading cadre.

"We prepared the formation of a Revolutionary Committee with great care. Earlier, before July, 1968, we had made various attempts to form a new management, but the discussion was not yet over, and it had proved impossible.

"Finally, on September 15, 1968, the Revolutionary Committee was formed, with Feng as chairman. It has been working for a year now, and shown itself competent. The masses have expressed their approval of the Revolutionary Committee. Our cadres are good. The masses regularly check up on the way the cadres are working and the work of the Revolutionary Committee. At regular discussions.

"We discussed the draft of the new Party statutes many times over. Both at Party meetings and at mass meetings. All this we went through with greatest care. We were all very happy about the outcome of these discussions. The new statutes are better than the old.

"We sent a representative to the Ninth Party Congress. He was a poor peasant from the Date Garden. He had been good in the living study and application of Mao Tse-tung Thought. The masses sent him to Peking. He was elected by the Party members. The masses aren't allowed to vote on Party questions. But they discuss things and utter their opinions. That's very important."

Kao Pin-ying:

"Some individuals wrote big character posters. Then at various levels, criticism of the cadres began. Errors were pointed out. Some people thought Feng hadn't been much good. He hadn't been following the revolutionary line.

Nor had he, they said, taken much part in manual work. But most were of the view that Feng was mainly all right. After all, he had been working for the revolution for several decades. Chairman Mao has taught us to assess a cadre on the basis of his history as a whole.

"Step by step those who had been criticized saw their errors. If the masses hadn't made their criticisms, they would never have seen them. And that's why the cadres dared to criticize themselves. After all, the cadres are there to serve the people. They must not be allowed to become our masters.

"I know what it was like, because I was criticized myself. At first I had a wrong attitude to these criticisms of my work. When people got up at the meetings and said I had not done this properly or done that properly and made mistakes here and made mistakes there, and that I hadn't followed the proper line, I was most distressed. I thought it all very unjust, after all my hard work. I thought the criticism was wrong. I found it hard to stand, hearing them talking out loud about me at the meetings. But I realized I really had made mistakes. And I read Chairman Mao. After all, we're the servants of the people. We must have the courage to accept public criticism. Only in this way could I find a better style of working. And that's why I must admit that, even if at first they seemed hard, these criticisms helped me. And when we'd discussed the whole matter thoroughly and I'd gone through my work and accepted being criticized and had criticized myself and realized my errors, then the masses gave me their confidence again and I was re-elected treasurer.

"At the beginning of the cultural revolution the big character posters started and many meetings were held to criticize the cadres. At these meetings the cadres also criticized themselves. There was a meeting every three days. Every single person in the entire brigade spoke up at them. Many times over. No one in the whole brigade remained silent. To begin with there were many who were unused to speaking. They had never spoken in public before.

"But as the cultural revolution went on, they all plucked up courage and expressed their views at the meetings. They understood that the cultural revolution could only be carried through if everyone said what was on his mind and presented his views in public.

"Since everyone has by now expressed his opinions, the number of meetings has been reduced. First, to one meeting every five days, then to one every ten days. Now we have study meetings twice a month. Today everyone is used to speaking in public, even the women.

"Before the cultural revolution, we cadres didn't really rely on the masses. We behaved as if we really knew best. At the meetings many sat silent, and we thought it was enough if we did the talking. After the cultural revolution, all this has changed. Now we rely on the people. Now it's the masses who are in power. In all important matters it is they who decide. They discuss everything. Today it is the masses who are leading developments.

"What has happened is right. Previously, even if all were formally directed by the Party, there were many parallel organizations. Now there is only the Revolutionary Committee. It is a unified leadership. It requires less administration. The masses can check up on the administration. The people have more power now. Today the masses speak their minds openly and have more to say about how things should be run than they did before. This is Chairman Mao's line.

Chi Chung-chou:

"Formerly, when the schools were run by the Education Office for Yenan hsien, teachers were moved hither and thither. That wasn't good. It's better for the children if

126

teachers remain where they are. I was a teacher at Yenan for a while. Now I'm back here at Liu Ling. Today, since the cultural revolution, it is the masses themselves who decide about the teachers. It's better this way.

"Throughout the year 1966–1967 cultural-revolutionary criticism was going on here at Liu Ling school. The revolutionary teachers and their pupils criticized the mistaken educational policy, policy in which school marks were crucial. We had been encouraging our pupils to study in order to get on in society. We were educating climbers and folk who wanted to become famous. That was all wrong.

"I know, because I always used to feel very happy, and regard it as a triumph for myself as a teacher, each time one of my pupils was accepted for Yenan Middle School. I did my best so that as many as possible should go on to higher studies; and this meant I was always giving the pupils more and more homework, driving them to work harder and harder. I thought I was doing this for their own good.

"I didn't bother my head about the principles laid down by Chairman Mao for school work. I was trapped in the ideologies of the past.

"Then, when all the criticism began, the pupils in my class got up, all of them, every single one, and criticized me. It was my star pupils who began it. And Li Chi-shen, who had gone on to Yenan Middle School and of whom I was so proud, came back and criticized me. Now he's a teacher here. But at the time, when they criticized me, I felt extremely bitter. I'd thought I was a good teacher. Now here were all my pupils, standing up, both the older ones and those I had just then, and criticizing me.

"I was not sufficiently conscious then. I didn't understand. Then my pupils began reading Chairman Mao with me and gradually I realized the mistakes I'd been making. Of course I wasn't a bad teacher, in the sense of having

127

neglected my teaching work or having beaten the pupils or shouted at them. But my work had had the wrong goals. I'd been trying to educate my pupils to become book-worms. Behind my errors lay a conviction about which I'd never really been clear. It lay within me. The notion that the educated man is superior. That the scholars must lead.

"This meant I'd really been trying to turn my pupils into spiritual aristocrats who would ride on the shoulders of the people. It took time before I perceived this. I could only perceive it by studying Chairman Mao and making comparisons with my own activities. Gradually I arrived at insight into my errors. I'd been driving my pupils to-wards a false ideal. An ideal which belonged to a feudal world of learned officials and oppressed masses. And this had been the real source of the pride I'd felt at being able to lead certain pupils on until they were accepted for Yenan Middle School.

"And in this work of mine I'd damaged many pupils by placing excessive demands on their lessons, excessive demands for intellectual work. I'd been leading one group of pupils to separate themselves from practical experience and real work, and depressing another group into re-garding themselves as inferior. Yes, I'd even managed to damage their health by giving them so much difficult homework.

"Of course I hadn't been doing all this consciously. I'd merely been following the general line in education at that time. Liu Shao-ch'i's line. But still it was I who had done it. It took some time before all this became clear to me. But by studying Chairman Mao with my pupils' help I realized that my task was to serve the people and was therefore able to go on with my work, this time with the full support and confidence of my pupils, all of us together.

"But there was another difficulty over all this criticism.

It is not so difficult to welcome correct criticism. What is in the way is really only false pride. And that's easily overcome. What was really hard was even to welcome criticism that was untrue, mere lies. That was very hard indeed. This is a problem one must see clearly.

"Certain pupils came with criticisms which were just lies. What they alleged simply wasn't true. But suppose I'd fought back? The fact was, my authority—an authority which, being based in spite of everything on feudal obedience and not on a proletarian consciousness, was a false authority—had taught my pupils to hold their tongues. They had never criticized me, not even to make such justifiable criticisms as I would have needed for my own development. When the cultural revolution came, and all the criticism began, and this false authority of mine was demolished, then certain pupils got up and criticized me without regard for the truth.

"Suppose I'd defended myself. I could have scared both them and the others into silence. But that would have been to silence the justifiable criticism, too. To help myself solve this problem I turned to Chairman Mao. And I perceived that I shouldn't fight back, but allow their criticism—even if not always true—free play. If we'd been making mistakes, I would learn from these criticisms, and if in reality I had not made any mistakes, then I would use even the erroneous criticism as a warning against making such mistakes in the future.

"Afterward, later on in the cultural revolution, when all the pupils had learned to speak up and criticize in the right way, our discussions clarified what was right and what was wrong, and I explained why such or such a piece of criticism against me had been wrong. I showed them that it didn't agree with the facts. But I had not used my authority as a teacher and an adult to fight back at my pupils. And that was important. Only in that way could they develop.

"As a teacher I enjoy a sort of authority now different from that which I had before the cultural revolution. For now we are working toward other goals. We aren't chasing high marks or driving ourselves to trying to educate so-called 'educated people.' Now we learn from each other."

Lo Han-hong:

"At the 1964 and 1965 meetings there was no criticism and very little discussion. The official policy was being followed. I suppose many people thought the leadership was too little interested in agriculture and too keen on getting into town and going to market. But no one said so.

"Then came the cultural revolution, with its big character posters and large discussions and everyone was to utter his or her opinion. Not being a cadre, I was not criticized. It was just that I'd become so absorbed in the noodle factory. There's so much to learn about noodles. I'd got hold of literature on noodle-making, too. And there were some who thought I was shirking the heavy work and burying myself in reflections on noodle-making. Yet no one criticized me. Though Mau Pei-hsin did say once that I wasn't exactly fond of hard work. So in 1967 I worked a great deal in the fields—especially as we didn't just then need so much labor in the noodle factory.

"By and by we came to the conclusion in the course of our discussions that the cadres were good and that on the whole they had rectified their mistakes and that we should again give them our confidence and let them go on being our leading cadres."

Liu Teh-ching:

"At first the cadres thought their mistakes had been trivial. They refused to accept our criticisms. So we read out quotations to them. We discussed matters with them. We showed them that it wasn't just a question of their mistakes, but of the implications of those mistakes, the direction in which they were leading. The whole line to which their mistakes added up. We youngsters held open-hearted meetings with the cadres, we got close to each other, and in this way helped each other to arrive at insight. Then the cadres turned to the masses and criticized themselves in front of them."

Ching Chung-ying:

"The criticism was important. Comrade Tsao had been responsible for agriculture. We older peasants didn't think he'd been much good. I supplied material for a big character poster and helped put it up. 'Comrade Tsao hasn't put politics first,' we wrote. 'Comrade Tsao has been following the wrong line and that's why agricultural output hasn't been too good, and our work hasn't yielded the results it should have.' Lots of people gathered and read this and everyone discussed it. We held big meetings and Comrade Tsao twice had to make self-criticism."

Tsao Chen-kuei:

"During the cultural revolution the whole management was criticized. The cultural revolution was led by Chairman Mao, and the poor and lower middle peasants rose and began to interest themselves in the State's affairs and discussed all sorts of questions. We'd done wrong. We were criticized for economic policy and for beginning to assume the airs of bureaucrats."

Li Shang-wa is married now. She married in 1966. She was twenty years old at that time.

"We'd known each other for two years when we got married. I myself chose to get married. He is from Yenan. He's the stoker at the bath-house. We've a daughter who is two. I work in the Fifth Labor Group."

Liang Shiu-chen is thirty-two, she's a member of the Revolutionary Committee. She says, "Li Shang-wa's marriage was a problem. We're trying to raise the age of marriage for girls. There have been no child-marriages within living memory. But we are actively propagating the idea that women should marry late. This gives them time to develop. We discuss this with the young girls and explain to them Chairman Mao's principle that young marriages aren't a good thing. Nowadays most of the girls are marrying at twenty-two, twenty-three, or twenty-four. It's better. But of course circumstances alter cases. And we had many discussions about Li Shang-wa.

"Her problem was that her father was in ill health. In her family there was only one person who was working, and that was Li Shang-wa. That made things hard for her. But when she got married her husband helped to take care of her father. Li Shang-wa and her husband liked each other and wanted to get married. The family's situation being what it was, it wouldn't have been right to discuss with them and suggest they postpone the wedding. But in principle, as a result of our information work and conversations with the girls, we have raised the age of marriage from 18 to 22, 23, 24, or so. But it's all a matter of information, not of law or compulsion.

"We continue both with our political and our information work on family planning. Condoms have become very much cheaper. There was a problem with Lo Han-hong. When he got married in 1963 he and his wife at once had children. Which is only natural. They had a son. But then, immediately afterwards, they had two more. And since then his wife hasn't been able to do any work except within the family. She's been pregnant and looking after little children the whole time. So when the third child was born, we women had a discussion with her. After all, it wasn't good for her. She agreed entirely. She thought it would be better for the mothers if families were planned. She wanted to plan her children and not be pregnant all the time.

"She spoke to her husband and he agreed. This was also partly because the men had had a frank talk with him. He understood the problem. And these talks help. These last two years Lo Han-hong's wife hasn't been pregnant.

"Nowadays a daughter has the same rights as a son. Formerly we had to fight hard for the equal rights of daughters. Under feudal custom the son was worth very much more. But we've left all that behind. No propaganda is needed any more. Now son and daughter are equals.

"During the cultural revolution we took a great stride forward. Formerly, meetings had mostly been attended by men. There had been some female activists, like Li Kuei-ying. When she moved with her husband to Yuling in 1964 I succeeded her on the brigade management committee as the person responsible for women's questions. But most of the activists had been men.

"This was one of the questions raised at the time of the big criticisms. It was Wang Hsiu-ying from the First Labor Group who raised it. That was in the spring of 1967. We condemned Liu Shao-ch'i's black line: that women are only capable of housework. Quoting Mao Tse-tung, we said that since we women are half of heaven we want to take part in all political activities and in all decisions, too.

"The brigade discussed this a great deal. Then the masses decided that men, too, were under an obligation to do their share of housework. At first some of the men got up and said we simply couldn't make such decisions. To look after children, that was woman's work. They were unwilling. They pointed out how children cry for their mummies at nights. They said it wasn't right, for the children's sake, for women to attend meetings while the men sat at home. It wouldn't be good for the children, they said.

"Then we women put the question to the brigade: are we, or are we not, to participate in political work? Many discussions followed. We also told the men it would be good for them to learn to look after children. Finally the brigade came to a unanimous opinion: it was decided that when the women go to meetings, the men shall stay at home and look after the children. In this way it wouldn't only be men who spoke at meetings and decided things."

(In 1962 there was only one woman among the twelve members of the brigade management committee; today, of the eleven members of the Revolutionary Committee, three are women.)

"The young intellectuals have been a great help. These young women from Peking, particularly, have influenced the brigade's young women. They sing and laugh and aren't a bit shy. They get up and make speeches. The most active women here are those who are between thirty and forty. The young girls find it harder to speak in public. But they, too, take part. The young intellectuals from Peking lead the work of getting the women to study Chairman Mao. They also teach them their songs. This has improved the atmosphere in the brigade. They're always striking up some song.

"All the women are studying Chairman Mao now. Studying hard, and applying what they've learned. This is very important. It's basic to our work. Work in production, both large matters and small. There aren't many quarrels and personal conflicts among us, but when they do arise, then we intervene and try to resolve them with the aid of Mao Tse-tung's thoughts. We had one example of just such a personal problem only the other day. It was Chang Yu-chen, in the Second Labor Group. She often got angry with her husband. Very. Nothing important. Just little things. But all the time they were having terrible quarrels. So we raised the question in the Revolutionary Committee.

"We sat down with Chang Yu-chen and her husband and read what Chairman Mao had written about the correct handling of contradictions among the people. When Chang Yu-chen and her husband had their quarrels these weren't a contradiction between ourselves and the enemy, but a contradiction among the people. So we tried to apply what we'd studied and had a deep, thorough-going discussion and a frank exchange of views with Chang Yu-chen and her husband. After that they stopped quarreling. They seem happy together. At least for the time being.

"That was one little matter we resolved with the help of Mao Tse-tung Thought. But of course there have been bigger ones. Since we have gotten ourselves a mill, household work isn't so heavy any more. But a lot of the work still falls on the women. This means a woman's day's pay is less than a man's and that they work fewer days. On an average the women do about 200 productive days' work a year. Chairman Mao has said,

With the rise of the peasant movement, the women in many places have now begun to organize rural women's associations; the opportunity has come for them to lift up their heads, and the authority of the husband

135

is getting shakier every day. In a word, the whole feudal-patriarchal ideology and system is tottering with the growth of the peasants' power.

He has also said:

> In order to build a great socialist society, it is of the utmost importance to arouse the broad masses of women to join in productive activity. Men and women must receive equal pay for equal work in production. Genuine equality between the sexes can only be realized in the process of the socialist transformation of society as a whole.

"The new mill is one factor in the women's liberation from heavy household work. But we also discussed what more could be done. We started with Chairman Mao's basic principle of self-reliance. After thorough study of Chairman Mao and proper dicussions we decided to establish a cooperative sewing house. It is women who sew the families' clothes and this is difficult, time-consuming work.

"In the spring of 1967 we turned to the brigade, and were given 2 mu of earth to cultivate. There we grew grain. With this grain we bought ourselves a sewing machine. Now we have three sewing machines. One man and two women are at work in the sewing-house. The man is a tailor, who knows about cutting. The women learn from him. It is the brigade which pays their wages and the brigade which provides the thread. We pay in work-points. They are discounted at the annual meeting. Trousers for an adult cost 2 work-points, a jacket for an adult costs 2.5 work-points. Trousers and jacket for a six-year-old together cost 2.5 work-points. Compare this with the time it takes if one sews children's clothes by hand — three days for trousers and jacket, i.e., about 18 work-points — and one can see how, by relying on our own resources, we have relieved women of one more aspect

136

of the burden of household work and made it possible for them to achieve greater equality."

Wang Yü-lan was thirty-nine. She was a member of the Revolutionary Committee: "I'd worked a lot in agriculture and showed myself industrious, so in 1965 I was elected to the board of management of the brigade. But I never spoke at meetings. I was selfish. I had my household and my children to look after. I thought of my own private interests and was not an active member of the board.

"No one criticized me during the cultural revolution. But from studying Chairman Mao I realized what a mistake I'd been making, to sit silent at the meetings of the management board, thinking of my own household instead of the affairs of the State. Before the cultural revolution women were too tied to their own homes. Then we discussed the importance of interesting ourselves in State affairs, just as much as the men do. During these discussions I became more politically aware.

"Now we women are studying Chairman Mao. We read newspapers and discuss things. Formerly it was only the men who discussed things when resting from their work in the fields. Now we women, too, talk things over. During the cultural revolution nine women have learned to read. But for the older of us, who never went to school, it's hard. The younger women study with us, though, and teach us from *Quotations from Chairman Mao Tse-tung*. The young women say we women must be capable of making up our minds and arriving at decisions. They say, too, that we women must study, so as to work efficiently. That's why they read with us and help us to understand the characters.

"My mother-in-law is very old. She is seventy. I have two girls who go to school. When they come home they read from *Quotations from Chairman Mao Tse-tung* to their grandmother. She is very happy about this. She

137

says, 'Maybe I'll soon be dead, but I'm glad I've been allowed to hear the voice of Chairman Mao.'

"Before the cultural revolution I never spoke at meetings of the brigade management committee. Sometimes I didn't even attend them. But now I take part in all discussions. If someone makes a suggestion, I state my opinion, like the others do, whether it's right or wrong. Now I discuss what crops are best to grow and what is not so good, and express my views.

The Young Intellectuals

The atmosphere in Liu Ling had changed. The city had come closer. Seven years ago the evenings had been still and quiet. But now people sang after nightfall. They played harmonicas and laughed and chatted all over the village. Down by the road voices could be heard, youngsters from Peking and Sian who were in the village to be re-educated. By their mere presence, they were changing the village.

Today intellectuals and city-dwellers of various sorts are out in the villages of China to be transformed by work and to be re-educated by poor peasants and lower middle peasants.

It is several years now since those who had moved to the cities returned to their home villages. People like Mau Pei-hsin who, on the instructions of the Party, left town and moved back. Out in the villages they constitute a most active force. Without holding any official position, Mau Pei-hsin is quite definitely one of the political and economic driving forces. It is around him—and around veterans of the People's Liberation Army like the doctor, Wang You-nan—that the youngsters of the village and the young intellectuals from Peking and Sian gather in the evenings for discussions.

Then there is a large group of responsible cadres and experts of various sorts who are currently working and studying out in the countryside. They are not there as a punishment. Nor are they there for good. They are there to be re-educated. They had been sitting in their offices playing the decision-maker and losing contact with Chinese realities. That the Western and Soviet press should call this a punishment I find interesting. These are people, after all, who have held positions of high responsibility. And I don't see anything penal in highly-placed politicians going back where they came from and finding out afresh how people live.

There are no such high cadres at Liu Ling. At Liu Ling there are only youngsters and students. Eighteen of them altogether. But they constituted two quite different groups, and were in Liu Ling on quite different errands.

One group consisted of graduates. They had just passed their exams. Five of them, three men and two women, one mathematician, one engineer, one economist, one agronomist and one teacher. All were receiving their regular monthly salary, 46 Y, from the State and were paying the brigade for their board and lodging. With the exception of the agronomist—who perhaps was going to remain in the district—they were all there for a year or so of re-education.

They were making themselves useful at Liu Ling. Under the leadership of the agronomist they had succeeded in producing the region's first crop of cotton. This piece of applied science meant that in future the agricultural workers of Liu Ling—and of nearby brigades—would be able to cultivate cotton. All earlier attempts in the district had failed. Either the cotton had frozen, if planted too early, or had been taken by the frost, if planted too late. The frost comes early at Liu Ling. As early as October 6 there are night frosts.

But these graduates hadn't come to Liu Ling to teach the peasants agriculture. They had come here to be re-educated through work, and so be able to solve such problems as the cotton problem.

Speaking of the importance of theoretical studies, Li Hai-tsai said, "As fruit-growing increases we need more

140

people who are specially trained at it. All questions are discussed at our meetings. We discuss fertilization. When it should be done, and how much. We discuss how we shall graft and how to prune. We have just come to the conclusion that the big apple trees must be manured twice a year. We have experience; we also need education.

"I had sent three of our members to a technical college for agriculture with its experimental station, here in the district. Now we have asked to send several more. The Revolutionary Committee has discussed the question, and three more are to be trained. First they learn what these three specialists which we already have know about insecticides and fertilizers and so forth. Then they are allowed to practice and learn at the experimental station. But their wages are no higher for that. Studies do not lead to higher wages for the same work. And all the time we connect this with the study of Mao Tse-tung Thought. All this has yielded good results. For even when they begin to study, these specialists of ours already know a lot.

"For those who have only been to school, it's different. They have studied and studied, but they didn't learn what they should have. As long as Liu Shao-ch'i's line prevailed, youngsters were studying in order to become officials. People who had studied and been to college were regarded as superior to those who hadn't. But today we have thoroughly broken with these false theories, as we showed in practice during the cultural revolution. We fetched home some students who had gone to the Agricultural College at Sian and who had been studying fruit-growing for several years and said to them: Now, here are the fruit trees, show us what you know!

"And they just stood there and couldn't do a thing. All they could do was to talk about their theories, and these theories were just a lot of empty words. When it came down to brass tacks, their theories were no use to them, and our own specialists, whom we had trained here at home, proved themselves to be their superiors.

"So I had a talk with these students. They admitted that they had been poisoned by the ideas of Liu Shao-ch'i, and had thought themselves superior to us just because they'd been to college and we hadn't. They'd come here as bureaucrats. But when we showed them what their knowledge was really worth, they realized it is impossible to transfer theories straight from the classroom into practice. They had to integrate themselves with the masses and learn how to work. Only then can their theories have any value.

"They weren't a bad lot. They criticized themselves and began to learn from us."

Old prejudices aren't easily rooted out. Even while the cultural revolution was still going on, many academic teachers told their pupils: "Remember—physical labor damages the brain." Old China had had the most ancient system of exams in the world. Once it was a model for Europe. By exam after exam the most competent were sorted out. Until in the end only the real élite, capable of ruling the country, remained. But of course the question is: What is meant by "capable"? In old China people used to show their capacity by a thorough knowledge of the classical culture and by being able to write formally perfect essays. The purpose of education was not to communicate knowledge. It was to shape character. No one who had gone through such an education should think "subversive" thoughts. He was therefore suitable to be an official in a bureaucratic-feudal society. And the old classical education was admirably adapted to this purpose.

Sometimes it is said that the old Chinese mandarin system gave even the poorest boy a chance. If only he studied and was clever, it is alleged, he could rise to the highest positions in the realm. This lie hardly has the merit of being beautiful.

For more than 2,000 years the ruling class were land-lords, they were the educated, they held political power as officials and from them descended all the scholars.

The Chinese exam system was an instrument by which the ruling landowner class could both keep itself in power and also control thought. After the liberation the sylla-buses were changed, but the system survived in new forms: the race for high marks, the exams, the tests, the university for the élite. And the results were precisely what might have been expected—it was the children of the former ruling class who were most successful, who got the highest marks, who got into the university, became experts, and were going to rule the country. No "injustice" was needed for power to be retained in the families which had held it for 2,000 years. All they needed were marks and exams.

Tian Yuan-chao from Peking, age eighteen, son of a motor mechanic, had been one of the first Red Guards in his school: the 131st Middle School. Now he had settled at Liu Ling. He had been what his teachers called a "brilliant pupil." But he said, "Marks used to be everything. They divided the pupils up into 'good' and 'bad.' The 'good' pupils with high marks were to go on to 'good' universities like Peking. The 'bad' pupils, with lower marks, would go on to 'bad' universities. All the teachers bothered about was marks. And the teachers wanted as many pupils as possible to get into the 'good' universities. For such success reflected glory on their teachers. To come by such glory they tried to force the pupils to get high marks. They were always demanding that the pupils write essays and giving them homework. But which pupils got bad marks, then? Most often it was the children of workers and peasants. It was they who got the low marks. The teachers did not care for them. No one reaped any glory from them. All this we criticized bitterly. It was Liu Shao-ch'i's line."

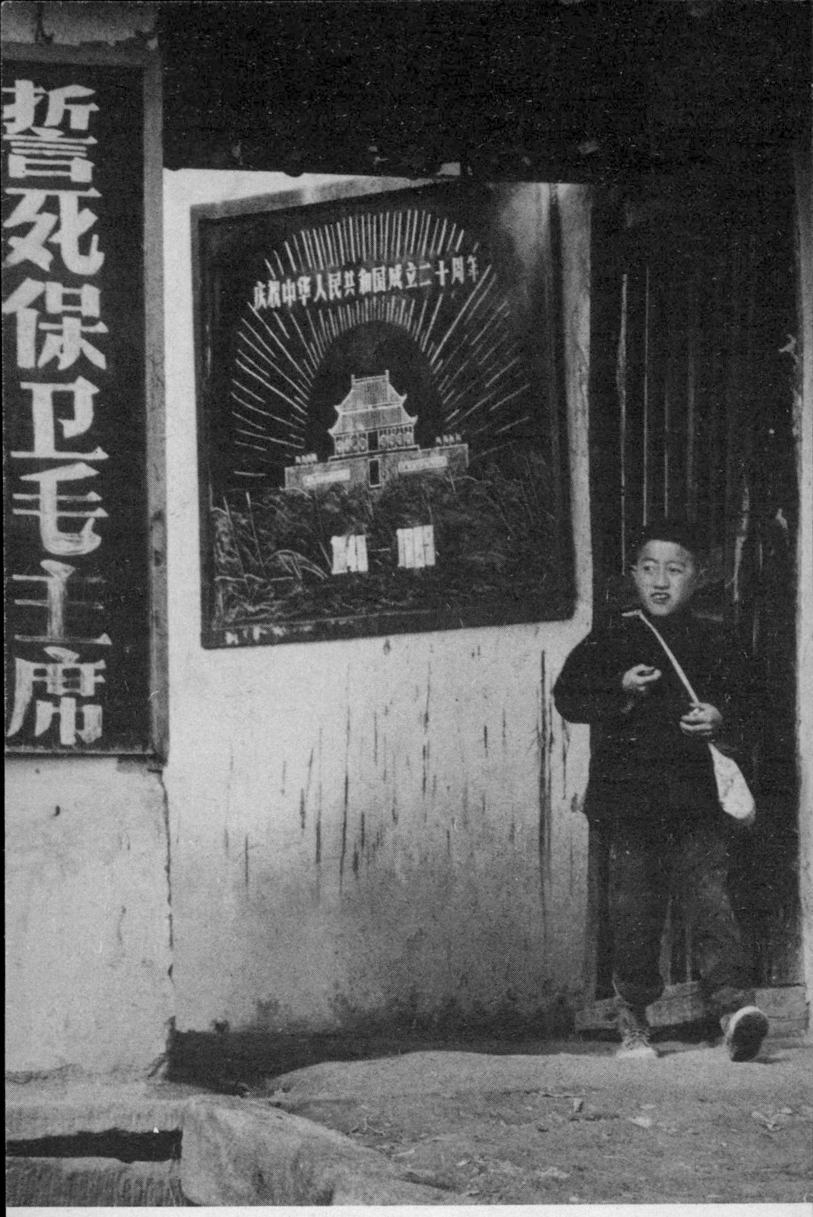
誓死保卫毛主席
庆祝中华人民共和国成立二十周年

Liu Ling School is now a unified seven-year school. The five first classes form an elementary school; classes six and seven are a lower middle school. This reform was carried out in October, 1968. Previously the school had had six classes.

The school has 268 pupils, from the entire brigade. Boys 168, girls 100. All the brigade's children go to school. Obligatory schooling has been enforced throughout the entire district. Before the cultural revolution, parents had to contribute to the costs of heating and providing drinking water (5.50 Y per school year). These fees have now been abolished; all that remains to pay is a teaching fee of 1 Y per pupil per term. It is hoped that this will be done away with shortly, too. The brigade is currently building new stone caves for the school.

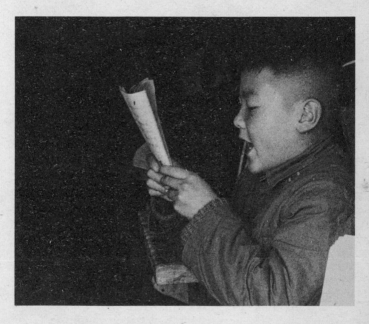

The school did not close during the cultural revolution, but between September, 1966, and January, 1967, its premises were used to provide accommodation for visiting Red Guards and for discussions between Red Guards, the pupils, and the teachers. Since January, 1967, instruction has continued according to plan.

149

The school was formerly subordinate to the Education Bureau at Yenan hsien. Now it comes under the Revolutionary Committee. All decisions, curricula, holidays, appointments of teachers, etc., are made by the Revolutionary Committee. The immediate management of the school is in the hands of a seven-man committee, under the chairmanship of Feng Chang-yeh, Chairman of the Revolutionary Committee. The person immediately responsible is the vice-chairman of the school committee, Hsueh Si-chun, who is chairman of the Poor Peasants and Lower Middle Peasants Association at Liu Ling, and also a member of the Revolutionary Committee. A representative of the pupils sits on the school committee, and also a teachers' representative. The latter is Liu Chen-jung, formerly head master (February, 1966, to October, 1968).

150

The post of head master was abolished when the school
was transferred from the Education Bureau to the
Revolutionary Committee. The school has ten teachers
and a cook. Eight of the teachers receive their salaries
from the State authorities. This salary is the same as it
used to be (calculated according to training and years
of service). The cook and two of the teachers—former
Red Guards who have been allotted teaching work, a
girl, Wang Shih-chieh, 20, and a boy, Li Chi-shen, 24,
son of Li Hsin-chen—are all paid by the brigade at
ordinary work-points. Currently it is being discussed
whether the other teachers, too, should not be transferred to the brigade, in which case the State would pay
the difference between the work-point wage rate and the
State salaries established earlier. Now that the school

has been taken over by the brigade, the teachers are no longer moved about the Education Bureau's district but, normally, remain in the same school. It also means there is no need to apply to the authorities for permission to give the pupils time off during the harvest.

Teaching methods are still under discussion. Various methods are being tried out experimentally. The basic principle is to tie up theory with practice. New school books are being tried out. But certain things have already been decided. All marks have been abolished. Also all homework. Pupils do not merely have the right to help each other when doing their exercises, etc.: they are under a positive obligation to do so. Everyone in the class moves up to the next class. Pupils who find study difficult are not kept back or expelled from the class. It is their comrades' and teachers' duty to help them. Pupils must not compete with one another—they should help each other. Competition, marks, and examinations lay the basis for a fundamentally wrong attitude to life.

The older among the poor peasants do their share of direct teaching. They teach the history of the class struggle and tell how things have developed at Liu Ling. When Hsueh Si-chun was teaching class-consciousness to the sixth class he also gave an account of Mao Tse-tung's speech at the Ninth Party Congress. As yet it has not been published. But the schoolchildren are discussing it.

The old pioneer organization had been dissolved. In its stead came the junior Red Guards. The reason given by Tsao Chung-fong, a teacher, was that the pioneer organization had been bureaucratic and authoritarian. Now the members elected their representatives directly. Previously they had been appointed from above. Another difference was that the junior Red Guards were guided by Mao Tse-tung's thought.

The school reform was new, so no pupils had yet left the seventh class. The question of their higher studies had not been decided. But the view was that, after finishing school, all pupils should go out and work in the brigade. No final exams or marks should be permitted. Afterward the poor and lower middle peasants (i.e., the youngsters' working mates in the labor group they belonged to) should decide which among them were suitable for higher education.

Mao Tse-tung's thought guides the school's work: *The length of schooling should be shortened, education should be revolutionized, and the domination of our schools and colleges by bourgeois intellectuals should not be tolerated any longer.*

To accomplish the proletarian revolution in education, it is essential to have working class leadership; the masses of the workers must take part in this revolution and, in cooperation with Liberation Army fighters, form a revolutionary three-in-one combination with the activists among the students, teachers and workers in schools and colleges, who are determined to carry the proletarian revolution through to the end. The workers' propaganda teams should stay permanently in the schools and colleges, take part in all the tasks of struggle-criticism-transformation there and will always lead these institutions. In the countryside, schools and colleges should be managed by the poor and lower middle peasants—the most reliable ally of the working class.

The attitude to youth is expressed in Mao Tse-tung's words: *The world is yours, as well as ours, but in the last analysis, it is yours. You young people, full of vigor and vitality, are in the bloom of life, like the sun at eight or nine in the morning. Our hope is placed in you. . . . The world belongs to you. China's future belongs to you.*

How should we judge whether a youth is a revolutionary? How can we tell? There can only be one criterion, namely, whether or not he is willing to integrate himself with the broad masses of workers and peasants and does so in practice. If he is willing to do so and actually does so, he is a revolutionary; otherwise he is a non-revolutionary or a counter-revolutionary. If today he integrates himself with the masses of workers and peasants, then today he is a revolutionary; if tomorrow he ceases to do so or turns round to oppress the common people, then he becomes a non-revolutionary or a counter-revolutionary.

Liu T -ching

ABOVE: Tung Yang-chen
RIGHT: TOP, Ching Chung-ying; BOTTOM, Li Shang-wa

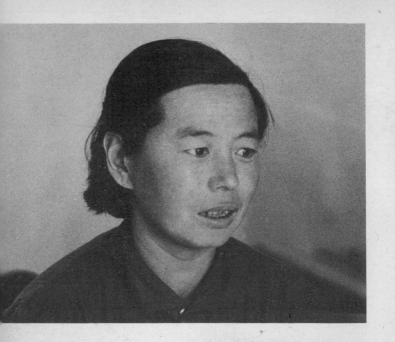

TOP ROW, LEFT TO RIGHT:
Chi Mei-ying, Tsao Chung-fong,
Mau Pei-hsin
RIGHT: Chi Chung-chou
BOTTOM ROW, LEFT TO RIGHT:
Li Chi-shen, Fu Hai-tsao,
Kiang Shu-ying, Tsao Chen-kuei

164

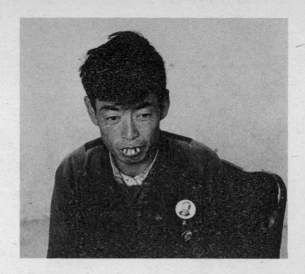

TOP ROW, LEFT TO RIGHT: Li Hai-yuan,
Li Hai-tsai, Chang Chung-liang
CENTER ROW, LEFT TO RIGHT: Liu Chen-jung,
Feng Chang-yeh
BOTTOM ROW, LEFT TO RIGHT: Wang Yu-lan,
Liang Shiu-chen, Ma Hai-hsiu

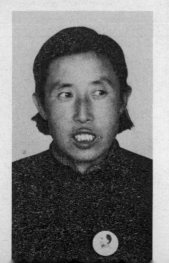

TOP ROW, LEFT TO RIGHT:
Mau Ke-yeh, Tian Yuan-chao,
Wang You-nan, Hsueh Si-chun
CENTER ROW, LEFT TO RIGHT:
Lo Han-hong, Kao Pin-ying
BOTTOM ROW, LEFT TO RIGHT:
Kao Yi-chin, Li Shiu-mei

During the cultural revolution the whole of this school system, with its race for high marks, its essay-writings and its obsession with exams, was smashed by the pupils. They had realized—just as Mao Tse-tung said—that a change of syllabus was not enough: the whole way of studying would have to be changed, if a new ruling class was not to seize power again.

The graduates were at Liu Ling to be re-educated by hard work. They were to be helped to overcome the notion that intellectual work is more respectable than manual work. For only by overcoming this would they be able to do any really intellectual work. They were to be helped to overcome the notion that it is harmful to work, to overcome the selfishness and self-absorption given them by the school, with its internecine struggle of every man's hand against his neighbor for high marks and degrees. They themselves wanted to come out into the villages. They had revolted against the school system and smashed it. Now they were to be transformed. To smash a bad examination system is not the same thing as to turn against studies. There was nothing "anti-intellectual" about this revolt. The revolution developed and the school was transformed from a school designed to meet the needs of a bureaucratic society into a school suited to the new society. The educational system now being built up all over China was based on the work once done at Yenan by Lin Piao, on lines laid down by Mao Tse-tung.

The second group of youngsters at Liu Ling consisted of five boys and eight girls from Peking. They were between seventeen and twenty years of age, and had gone through Middle School. Now they had moved to Liu Ling. They were going to stay for good. They were to become brigade members. Feng Chang-yeh said, "It's a bit troublesome for them to begin with, but it turns out all right in the end. At first they knew nothing and had difficulty in working. Now things are going better. Many were homesick. After all, they'd left their families behind. So we see to it that those really homesick go home and visit the families. After they come back, their homesickness is gone. The first year they get no work-points. That would be unfair, for they know nothing. It takes some time to learn how to work. To begin with, if they had been obliged to live on what they were entitled to from the work they'd done, they wouldn't have managed.

"That's why the State compensates the brigade for their food and lodging. The brigade gets about 200–300 Y for each of them during the first year. Additionally, the State pays each of the youngsters 10 Y in pocket money a month.

"But they're beginning to come on well and at our next annual meeting we're going to propose that they are awarded work-points and become ordinary members."

Ching Chung-ying said, "Youngsters from town have to learn everything from the ground up. When they first come here they know absolutely nothing. So we see to it that they take part in all sorts of work. They work in the vegetable-growing labor group and in the fruit orchard, they fetch manure, they work in the noodle factory, they work on the harvest and threshing and on the construction work. In this way they get an all-round knowledge of agricultural techniques.

"They have had difficulties to overcome. We fetch human excrement from the town latrines. Many of the town youngsters found this hard at first. They had to overcome their aversion to working in the latrines. They were quite simply afraid of human excrement. Afterwards they learned to do this work, became good at it; and now it's no longer any problem. They've changed because they wanted to change."

Mau Ke-yeh said, "These students, they come to me and want me to tell them things. They want to hear all about the revolution here in northern Shensi. They want to hear about Hu Tsung-nan. They've come here to learn from our experience."

Liu Teh-ching said, "We try to help them strike real roots here. At first they tended to wander about and brood on their families. We solved this problem by discussing it on the ideological level. There were some youngsters who found it hard to work. Some didn't dare go up into the hills and work. They thought it was too much like hard work. We studied Mao Tse-tung Thought together and after they had read about Comrade Bethune and his devotion to others and his unlimited feeling of responsibility toward his work, they were able to overcome their wrong attitude to working up in the hills. For what is there to working in the hills compared with leaving one's country and traveling half-way across the earth to sacrifice oneself unselfishly for the Chinese people, as Comrade Bethune did?

"After a year, their attitude has changed. They are close to the masses here. Nor is this something they just say. They show it in action. When the children are ill, they look after them as if they were their own brothers and sisters. They have a feeling for the collective property and are part of the brigade. That's why they're to be given work-points and be the same as everyone else."

These young people from Peking have come to Liu Ling to stay. Not for a month and not for a year, but for a lifetime. They will settle down there. Be changed by it. But they are also helping to change the village all about them. Together with Mau Pei-hsin and the village's own youngsters they are already a driving force, influencing developments.

The town has come closer. During the cultural revolution, the village's horizon—still limited seven years ago to the nearest provinces—was extended to China as a whole. Seven years ago only a few people had even been to Sian, the provincial capital. Today the village's isolation has been broken down.

These youngsters had asked to come here to the old liberated area. It has been said — in the West — that they were forced to. That they were really unwilling. Well, China is a big country, and I suppose there must have been some who didn't want to move out to the villages. But they are not many. For it would really and truly be to misunderstand young people not to see that just this sort of life at Liu Ling is attractive. That it is a great freedom.

Kiang Shu-ying was eighteen. She said, "When I graduated from Middle School I applied to the school's revolutionary committee to be allowed to come here. Everyone in my class was going out into the country. They applied for different places. We had seen them on our long marches. I'd been here. I wanted to get back. Again and again I applied, and in the end got permission. In changing our country we are changing ourselves. We take off our fine clothes and put on rough working clothes. We are learning from the poor and lower middle peasants here at Liu Ling. We are learning how to work, and we are learning what the revolution really is. We are also propagating Mao Tse-tung Thought. We help the old women learn to read. We read to them. We are here to become agricultural workers of a new sort."

What is happening in China just now is that the cultural barriers which used to separate "intellectuals" from "ordinary people" are being broken down, like the barriers which used to separate town from country. At Liu Ling youth is being converted and transformed. But they are also bringing new ideas with them, and transforming Liu Ling.

"We Rebelled"

Li Shiu-mei was twenty-five. She was from Fuping and had graduated from the Northwest China Institute of Economics and Finance at Sian. She had specialized in bank business and international economics. She had passed her exam and was now at Liu Ling to be re-educated by work.

"It was June 3, 1966, that we started the cultural revolution in our institute. It was then we heard that Peng Chen had been dismissed as mayor of Peking. We were very happy about this and immediately organized a demonstration. We demonstrated outside Party headquarters in Sian and shouted: 'Down with the handful of Party persons in power taking the capitalist road.' We could see them behind the windows. This was a big demonstration outside the Party headquarters.

"Next day a working group of Party representatives came to our institute. They were frightened and struck back at us, hard. They called us counter-revolutionaries and said our demonstration was hostile to the Party and that there were evil agents among us.

"They used the whole authority of the Party against us. But we gathered again in the classrooms and discussed the whole matter thoroughly. Having done so we found we were in the right. Then we understood that there must be something seriously wrong with the Party organization at Sian.

"The working group tried to lock us in and prevent us from contacting other students at other schools. So we barricaded ourselves inside our classrooms and read Chairman Mao. The Party representatives were not acting according with Mao Tse-tung Thought. We studied the quotations very closely and then opened fire on the Party representatives and showed them up for what they were. We rebelled.

"We wrote big character posters against the working group from the Party. Our entire institute became a sea of posters. We organized ourselves in little groups and took the whole question up point by point and thoroughly unmasked them.

"After we had rebelled and united the whole institute—with the exception of a little clique which followed the capitalist road—we were able to throw the working party out of the institute. We drove them out. They fled. We were educating ourselves in making revolution.

"Then came the Sixteen Points.* We were so happy that we cried. Chairman Mao's heart was with us. We had thought so all along, but now we knew it. After that we began to exchange experiences with other revolutionary groups and all monsters fled."

Kiang Shu-ying, eighteen, had graduated from Middle School in Peking and was now living in Liu Ling: "It was in early 1966 I'd got hold of *Quotations from Chairman Mao Tse-tung;* immediately my comrades and I began reading them. There was so much in them we'd never heard before. But the school authorities tried to suppress us. They didn't want us to read Chairman Mao on our own, didn't want us to have discussions on our own: all they wanted us to do was to get high marks and go on to 'good' universities.

"But we went on reading *Quotations from Chairman Mao Tse-tung.* Then we began to ask our teachers and

*The Sixteen Points: The Central Committee's resolution of August 8, 1966, which drew up the main directives of the cultural revolution and supported rebellious students.

173

the school management why they weren't acting in accordance with Mao Tse-tung Thought. We asked why so many things happened which did not accord with Chairman Mao's words. How could this be, when the teachers were always talking about Chairman Mao? Then they summoned us for interrogation. They said, 'You are dogmatic.' They forbade us to read Chairman Mao on our own. There must always be a responsible teacher with us, they said. But we ignored their prohibitions and went on studying *Quotations from Chairman Mao Tse-tung.*

"At first there weren't many Red Guards in the school. We'd organized ourselves into small groups, but we didn't begin calling ourselves Red Guards until we heard from other schools that they had formed the Red Guard. After we'd done so, the Party committee sent a working group to us. It forbade us to leave the school, it forbade us to discuss things with people on the streets, it forbade us to put up big character posters on the streets. It suppressed the great freedoms. Then we rebelled against them. They called us anti-Party and little dogmatics. We held great debates in the school. I took part. We said, 'We are Chairman Mao's Red Guard and we're in rebellion against everything false and wrong.'

"Then the working group kept us locked up in the school, so that we shouldn't get out into the streets to meet people and talk to them. And the working group trampled on us and said we'd understood nothing, because we were too young. But we replied that right and wrong are not matters of being old or young. He who is young may be right and he who is old and in authority may be wrong. They were adults and they came from the Party and they were in authority and held important positions, and we were young. But who was right and who was wrong could only be decided by a proper discussion. And we read Chairman Mao and we pointed out to them all the mistakes they were making.

174

"No one came and told us how we were to act. There were no orders. No one was our responsible leader. But we had got hold of *Quotations from Chairman Mao Tse-tung* and we read Chairman Mao and discussed in detail what he had said, and how right and wrong are not questions to be decided by word of command. We knew we were doing right in rebelling against the working group from the Party, for they were not acting in accordance with Mao Tse-tung Thought. Anyone could see that for himself, by studying Chairman Mao. We knew we were doing the right thing and that Chairman Mao was with us, for we had read his writings which our teachers had tried to keep from us and suppress, and we had discussed them in detail.

"Then, after August 16, 1966, when Chairman Mao received the Red Guards, our numbers increased, and the waves of revolution ran ever higher."

Li Chi-shen, twenty-four, who is the son of Li Hsin-chen and in 1962 was attending Middle School at Yenan, was now back at Liu Ling again. He was a teacher in Liu Ling School and teaching fifth class language and second class mathematics, and was also physical education teacher for all the classes: "Since 1961 I'd been attending Middle School at Yenan. It was a boarding school. I was a member of the board of the base organization of the Youth League in the school. In the spring of 1966 we were organizing criticism of the reactionary films and novels. All this was really in preparation for the cultural revolution.

"It was at the beginning of 1966 I got hold of *Quotations from Chairman Mao Tse-tung*. Since April we had been spreading it among the members of the Youth League. In June it could be bought in the bookshop at Yenan.

"After August 18, 1966, we organized ourselves into a Red Guard. The masses educated themselves and all leaders were elected from below. It was on August 20 we organized ourselves. I was not elected to anything. But

175

quite a lot of my comrades from the Youth League were. When we began, we were 400. Then we organized all the 1,000 pupils of our school. To begin with we had been somewhat restrictive. That was wrong.

"We criticized the wrong methods in our school. We sent out propaganda groups to discuss things with people. What we chiefly discussed was that class struggle continued under socialism. We pointed out the danger of various hostile elements digging themselves in in the State apparatus and of the dictatorship of the proletariat being turned into a bourgeois dictatorship. We pointed to the way things had gone in the Soviet Union. We propagated Mao Tse-tung Thought. We went out into the villages and straight into the administrative organs in town and started discussions. We used our school as a base from which we spread out in every direction. We sent groups of Red Guards to various parts of the country. By our propaganda work we helped to raise the poor and lower middle peasants and workers to criticize.

"We organized ourselves into groups which made long journeys about the country. During these journeys we met comrades from various parts of the country and we held discussions and learned from each other.

"After these journeys we went out into the factories to integrate ourselves with the masses. I went to the tractor station in Yenan. In the daytime I worked, and in the evenings I made revolution. All our groups worked in this way. After a month we returned to school to complete the cultural revolution inside the school. It was then I was elected secretary of the school's brigade of Red Guards. My chief task was then to organize the reception of all the thousands of Red Guards who were coming to Yenan.

"We had established a network of reception stations all over the country. Those Red Guards who were to make long marches were to take money and coupons with them.

176

But not all of them did; and many practical problems had to be solved. Some 40,000 people live in this district. But at times there were 80,000 Red Guards here at once. Altogether, more than 600,000 Red Guards came to Yenan in the course of their long marches. And of course there were a lot of practical questions to work on.

"Now I'm propagating Mao Tse-tung Thought here at Liu Ling. It's not just a matter of reading out some quotations. One has to explain what the words mean and their general implications and to explain the whole line of thought and apply the quotation in practice."

Wang Shih-chieh, twenty, has graduated from Yenan Middle School. Now she was a teacher at Liu Ling School. She took fourth class, "We made our second long march in January, 1967. There were nine of us in the group. Both boys and girls. We'd told the committee in our school that we were going to Peking and had been given a letter of introduction from them. We went eastwards. It was winter and cold. We crossed the Yellow River and went on through Shansi. When we crossed the Wutai mountain there was a snowstorm and people said it was impossible to get over. But our wills were like iron. We held up *Quotations from Chairman Mao Tse-tung* and shouted out quotations at the mountain, as the storm howled all around us. We shouted, 'Be resolute, fear no sacrifice, and surmount every difficulty to win victory.'

"In this way we got across the mountain in the winter storm and came to the province of Hopeh. There we heard that Chairman Mao was going to receive the Red Guards in a few days' time. We were in despair. We'd never get to Peking in time to be received by Chairman Mao. So they sent trucks to pick us up. And we got to Peking in time. That time we stayed there for twenty days. Then the long marches came to an end and finally they sent us back to Yenan in trucks."

Kao Yi-chin, engineer. He was in Liu Ling to be re-educated. He had been a member of the Party since 1964 and had been secretary of the base organization of his college Youth League when the cultural revolution broke out: "The Party members were better trained ideologically. And that was why it was they who took the initiative in forming the Red Guard and who roused the masses to criticize. At my college there were ten of us who began to organize the Red Guard. But this didn't automatically make us its leaders. All leaders, at all levels, were elected by the masses.

"It was in 1965 that we got *Quotations from Chairman Mao Tse-tung.* It was distributed within the Party. Later it was spread within the Youth League, and by and by appeared in the bookshop.

"In September, 1966, I was elected to the leadership of the Red Guards in my college. Then I was sent as our representative to Peking. I arrived there in company with Red Guards from various parts of the country. There we were received by Chairman Mao. We also had a meeting with comrades from the Central Committee. Chou En-lai and Chen Po-ta spoke with us and gave us very important instructions from Chairman Mao. We had to unite with the workers and poor peasants. On their own the students cannot be victorious. Youth must go out to factories and agriculture. I was our college's delegate at this meeting. After that we went to all parts of China and exchanged experiences with Red Guards in various places.

"I made two long marches. We were seven in our group. We planned our routes. There was no anarchy. Even if some just went off. The second journey we made on foot. Then we went to Chengtu and Chungking. We went on foot because Mao Tse-tung had urged us to learn from our journeys and really walk through the country.

"The cultural revolution was a lengthy process. In July, 1967, we were able to set up a Revolutionary Committee in our college. But it was different in different places. Where the situation was good there was no need for a seizure of power. But in some places it was necessary to seize power from the handful of Party persons in power who were going the capitalist road.

"In Sian itself there was a delay in forming a Revolutionary Committee. There were difficulties. We were sent to different units to help them with the cultural revolution. We were sent as representatives with mandates from our own committee. Without written mandates it was impossible. The class enemy, one must never forget, was active and always trying to worm his way in. I was sent to the Party committee in Sian. I was one of a group whose task it was to help them with the cultural revolution and try to see that criticism was made in the right way. It was not our task to lead the work. We didn't come as superiors. Our task was to help people criticize the leadership. We criticized the Party leadership at Sian because it wasn't following Chairman Mao's revolutionary line."

Ma Hai-hsiu said, "There was a big change when the Red Guards came here in August, 1966. They came on foot from Peking and many other places. They propagated Mao Tse-tung's ideas and read out many articles to us and told us what was happening in the country.

"Five youngsters were living with me. They all came from Peking. They were polite and helpful. They asked me a lot about my life. They wanted to learn from me and the other old poor peasants.

"One can say that the cultural revolution in Liu Ling began with the Red Guards. They came here and talked to us and asked about everything in the village and read Mao Tse-tung to us, and we were able to compare Mao Tse-tung's words with reality.

"The Red Guards helped us to organize meetings at which we could take up all matters and say whatever we

179

liked, so as to arrive in this way at what was right and what was wrong. With their help we took up the practical issues.

"The biggest question which arose right from the outset was the question of vegetable production."

China: The Revolution Continued

It is evening and cold when Liu Teh-ching is to come back. She has been in Peking for the twentieth anniversary. Now she has phoned from Hwangling, saying she's on her way home.

All the school benches have been carried out into the schoolyard. Tsao Chen-kuei and Hsueh Si-chun are putting out the benches. Arranging them in row after row. Mau Pei-hsin has arranged the lighting. He has run his cables across the yard. Now the electric bulb is hanging over the speaker's table. It sways in the night breeze. He has put up the loudspeaker and Tsao Chung-fong is trying out the microphone.

Chairman Mao's portrait has been put up behind, and from all the villages of the brigade people are gathering in the schoolyard. Even the geologists from Sian, who are doing experimental work beyond the village of Hutoma, have come. They are waiting for Liu Teh-ching.

She is a young girl. She graduated from Liu Ling elementary school in 1962. She is from Hutoma village. Even before the cultural revolution she was one of the activists in the Youth League. During the cultural revolution she was one of the most active critics. She was one of those who initiated the criticism of Feng Chang-yeh and Tsao Chen-kuei. Now she is deputy Party secretary and member of the brigade's Revolutionary Committee: "Formerly I used to criticize the cadres. Now I'm a cadre myself, and I find I, too, become impatient and speak to people in the wrong tone of voice. That was one of the things we criticized most. The cadres were hard. They spoke harshly to people. They gave orders. They were rude. But now I notice that I, too, get impatient and irritable when things go slowly.

"The masses have criticized me for this. It has been said I lack the capacity for patient political work. But this is not destructive criticism. People tell me of these shortcomings to help me. They are magnanimous and forgiving.

"I criticized the cadres. Now I'm a cadre myself and get criticized. But the difference is that in those days the cadres were separating themselves from the masses. Now the masses exercise control over the cadres. And therefore their criticism nowadays is friendly and helpful. I know, too, that I make many mistakes because I am young. But the masses are keeping an eye on us cadres and help us when we begin to make mistakes or behave like officials. It's so terribly easy to get impatient and bad-tempered and to begin giving orders and pushing people around. That's why the masses must keep an eye on the cadres all the time. Power mustn't be allowed to slip out of the hands of the people."

Now, in the cold autumn darkness we are all waiting for her. In the night wind the electric light bulb swings to and fro and the schoolyard is packed with people. We smoke and chat. Liu Teh-ching has been the brigade's delegate in Peking during the twentieth anniversary celebrations. Three times she has seen Chairman Mao. Once she has spoken with Chou En-lai. She has been a long time at Peking and has seen a lot. All this she has telegraphed home. The telegram has been written up in big characters on the brigade notice board.

When she arrives they beat on drums. She has got off the bus at the main road and begun walking towards the village. A little boy has been keeping watch down there by the road. When the bus stopped and Liu Teh-ching got off, he ran to the village to tell us. As she crossed the bridge everyone began beating the drums. She is welcomed with a speech and the schoolyard is a seething cauldron of people. She goes up to the microphone: "I've seen Chairman Mao. He's in excellent health!"

Everyone cheers. They sing the *Song of the Helmsman*. Liu Teh-ching reports to the members of the brigade. Ten thousand delegates from all over China had been invited to Peking for the twentieth anniversary celebrations. From the province of Shensi thirty of them had been invited to stay with Chairman Mao in Peking.

"He doesn't live in luxury. He lives simply. He doesn't grow flowers in his garden. He grows maize and Chinese cabbages. In his personal life, too, Chairman Mao is a model for us poor peasants and lower middle peasants."

This cold autumn night a girl is speaking in a schoolyard among the loess hills of Shensi. She is a girl from Hutoma village. Her face is illumined by the twenty-five-watt lamp. The bulb is hanging from a wire hung between the school huts. It sways in the wind and the girl is talking about Chairman Mao and everyone is listening: old men grown thin and bony from hard work, school children, housewives, young people. And the girl is not talking about Chairman Mao in the abstract. She is reporting to the members who sent her. She tells them about visits to factories and schools, about discussions with various delegates, about meetings with various members of the Central Committee and what questions had been asked and how they were answered. This is no empty ceremony. It's a report to the members who sent her.

From all this, out in the barren inland of China, one can see how deep the revolution plows. And it is here— in a schoolyard among the loess hills, late one autumn evening—that China's future is being decided.

China is no "underdeveloped" or "backward" country. This time we visited industries and scientific institutions.

In dust-free halls—they were manufacturing semicon-
ductors for telecommunications and in the observatory at
Nanking young researchers showed us Chinese-built
satellite-tracking apparatuses which are automatically
charting the espionage satellites' paths over China. In
field after field China is now trying to reach—and sur-
pass—the international level in sciences and technology.

But China was an exploited and ravaged land, where
the great mass of the people were oppressed in misery
and want. And it is there, among the hundreds of millions
of Chinese out in the villages, that the great issue of
whether the Chinese Revolution is capable of being
carried through to the end, or whether it is to degenerate
and exude a thin deposit of privileged power-holders on
top of an oppressed mass, is being decided.

The old people of the village had told us about their
former miseries—but also how hard it had been for them
to rise and fight these poverty stricken conditions. The
revolution had not been simple, nor had it followed a
straight line. (See *Report from a Chinese Village*.) They
had told us about their victory—but also of its many vic-
tims. And every bit of progress after the victory of 1949
has been made only as a result of a struggle to overcome
difficulties and conflicts.

But this struggle, these difficulties and conflicts, have
not been an isolated phenomenon, either in the village of
Liu Ling or in the district around. Conditions could vary.
People were different in different parts of China. But the
basic traits were the same.

The villages had been isolated. In 1962 old Doctor Kao
had told us his memories from the fall of the empire:
"Then we were told that from now on we were called the
Republic of China and that the Ching Dynasty was at an
end. That was all. We were old country people and we
seldom went into the town and never talked about such
things as the emperor or government. Nobody would

184

have dared do that. And we never saw them either. The officials in the nearest yamen watched over us, and they were the same after the revolution as before it."

It was the social revolution which broke down this isolation. In 1962 the Old Secretary, Li Yiu-hua, told us of meetings in the thirties: "We held a lot of political mass meetings at that time. We had meetings about the Soviet Union, and at these meetings cadres came and told us that we had learned from Soviet experience how to make a revolution. The Soviet Government had also begun with only a few rifles. We had meetings at which we talked of how all humanity was to be freed of all oppression and all misfortune, and how all peoples were to become as brothers and live as equals, all over the world. We had meetings about imperialism and what the imperialists had done in China."

Today, too, meetings were being held about international questions. Meetings in support of the Vietnamese people in their people's war against the aggressors from the United States. Meetings about Albania, meetings about Palestine. But it wasn't only meetings. More important was that in the discussions of the problems in Liu Ling they used comparisons and examples from abroad. When people at Liu Ling discussed the two lines, developments in the Soviet Union were taken to exemplify how things could turn out if the people lost their grasp on their own revolution.

Feng Chang-yeh said, "We're working for the world revolution. We aren't working for ourselves, we aren't only working for our own collective, we aren't only working for China: we're working so that all the peoples of the world shall be free, and other peoples' struggle is a struggle for our future."

This wasn't something which only Feng Chang-yeh said. It was being said in different ways by everyone. Nor was it just empty phrases. By the revolution and the

185

cultural revolution Liu Ling had broken down the village isolation and taken the step out into world politics.

Twenty years had passed since the nationwide victory. Yet the landowner class, overthrown at that time, still had not accepted its defeat. Li Hsiu-tang's wife—whose father-in-law once owned the entire valley, whose brother had had Tung Yang-chen's father beheaded and himself had been executed after the liberation—now walked down the village street dressed in silk and wearing golden earrings. Every step she took was a demonstration. When people saw her coming they looked straight through her.

Nor had Li Hsiu-tang himself given up. In the spring of 1967 he and his oldest son had cursed the peasants. Until then they had believed they would recover their power. The son, Li Ta-min, age twenty-two, had cursed Ching Chung-ying and said, "Damnation upon you and all poor peasants. This land belongs to us. For twenty years, all my life, you've been oppressing me. But the land is mine."

Landowners never forget that they used to own the soil. And as late at 1962, Li Hsiu-tang was still hoping his family was going to recover its power by peaceful means. It was his children who were going on to a higher education. It was he who had married off his daughter to the secretary of the brigade Youth League, Lo Han-hong. He was beginning to make connections once more.

During the cultural revolution all this had changed. Most of his children had disavowed him and drawn a sharp line of distinction between themselves and their parents. It is not so that in China people are condemned to their class origin.

"No one can choose his origins. But the line he follows, that's something he *can* choose."

If he draws a sharp line and honestly opposes his family, and takes a correct stand, even the child of the counter-revolutionary is accepted.

No one is judged by the actions of his parents: but by his own actions. And this goes for the children of counter-revolutionaries just as much as for the children of revolutionary heroes.

The responsible cadres in the brigade had not been real enemies of the revolution in the same way as Li Hsiu-tang's wife who, every time she showed herself, demonstrated against the revolution and the power of the poor peasants. Every step she took down the village street, dressed in silk and wearing golden jewelry, was a demonstration against the collective. No one turned his head to look at her. No one said a word to her. Her demonstration was futile; thus she was not suppressed by force.

But the responsible cadres had entered a road which, step by step, was leading away from the revolution. They weren't capitalists. Nor did they desire capitalism. But they had begun to follow a road that led to the people losing their grip on the State. Capitalism would be peacefully restored in China.

What makes Mao Tse-tung so important that he can be regarded as the third in line with Marx and Lenin is that he raised and solved the problem how, after the revolution, the people can secure the revolution. How the revolution can be continued under the dictatorship of the proletariat. How the revolution can be prevented from degenerating, leaving the people what they were before: an oppressed mass. The reason why, after Stalin's death, Khruschev was able to enter the path he did, was that people of the Soviet Union did not have a real grasp on the State, had lost the power to make political decisions to the technocrats and bureaucrats, and therefore could not exercise surveillance over its leaders.

At Liu Ling the victory of the cultural revolution had meant that the masses took back the power which the "apparat" had begun to wheedle out of their hands. Administration had been simplified. Investments had increased. There had been a change in income distribution. Security had become greater. The health insurance reform had been carried through. Production had grown and with its growth, the people's standard of living had risen.

Ching Chung-ying said, concerning the growth in vegetable production, "People's way of thinking has changed, and the fields bear a richer harvest."

Some "experts" take such utterances as evidence for their own statement that the Chinese Communists are not Marxists. But the whole question is more complex than that.

After the victory of the revolutionary armies, when the People's Republic had been declared, the land distributed, the landowners driven out and socialism had become possible, there remained—and still remain— millennia of class-rule in the form of habits, thoughts, traditions, and concepts in people's minds. These are often called "human nature." It is said: "People will always fight. It's human nature." It is also said: "Charity begins at home. Everyone looks after Number One."

Such notions don't change in a day. But they are not "human nature." They distort and entangle all growth, inhibit all that is being built up. The peasants used to say: "The Phoenix wasn't hatched in a chicken-run." And: "Wealth and sons are given by fate." Such proverbs helped Li Hsiu-tang and his wife to go on hoping that they would one day be able to recover their family's traditional power through their children. This way of thinking constituted a mighty force, tending to disrupt socialism. It was creating contradictions among the workers. For if—as the proverb said—everyone thinks of himself, then no investments could be made. And that would have meant that the collective would have fallen apart, into rulers and ruled. To realize that this is so is not un-Marxist. Marx himself realized it. Those who believe that Marx was some kind of economic determinist simply have not read Marx. Take the well-known sentences from *The Eighteenth Brumaire of Louis Napoleon:*

> Men make their own history, but they do not make it just as they please; they do not make it under circumstances chosen by themselves, but under circumstances directly encountered, given and transmitted from the past. The tradition of all the dead generations weighs like a nightmare on the brain of the living . . . The social revolution of the nineteenth century cannot draw its poetry from the past, but only from the future. It cannot begin with itself before it has stripped off all superstition in regard to the past.*

Mao Tse-tung has consistently pointed to this. In 1937 he wrote:

> True, productive forces, practice and the economic base generally play the principal and decisive role; whoever denies this is not a materialist. But it also must be admitted that in certain conditions, such aspects as the relations of production, theory and the superstructure in turn manifest themselves in the principal and decisive role . . . When the superstructure (politics, culture, etc.) obstructs the development of the economic base, political and cultural change become principal and decisive.

Proverbs cannot be combated by administrative means. No administrative apparatus is a weapon against a joke. Nor can a figure of speech—influencing the way people think and therefore having power over society—be combated with policemen, night sticks, and concentration camps. On the contrary, if used, it is precisely by undermining the power of the people that these administrative apparatuses, these policemen and night sticks and con-

*Karl Marx and Frederick Engels, *Selected Works* Vol. I (Moscow, Foreign Languages Publishing House, 1951), pp. 225, 227.

centration camps, endow the reactionary ideas with real material power. Even if the Chinese did not know it before, they could see it in the Soviet Union.

If socialism was to be made secure, a struggle had to be fought in people's minds. It was imperative that people become conscious of the entire tradition inherited from dead generations which, like a nightmare, was oppressing their minds. That they should be able to see and become conscious of the historical origins of these notions and their contemporary implications.

It was imperative that by talking things over people should make themselves conscious of what was right and what was wrong in the old traditions. And that they should become clearly aware that the tradition which was "right" for Li Hsiu-tang (because it could help his family to recover their power) was wrong for Ching Chung-ying. That right and wrong must be assessed not only in their historical context, but also their class context.

In the class society the rulers talk a lot about "human nature" and "efficiency" and "profitability." These are abstract generalized concepts. And if they are held to be valid, it is because society is split up into mutually conflicting classes. General concepts then become nothing more than an expression of the rulers' particular needs.

To these generalized notions must be opposed the new liberating ideas. That is why, in China, the revolutionaries have taken up the struggle against "human nature" and against "love" and against "beauty." Not because they are "against" love or beauty; but because these concepts, in their generalized formulation, become falsified, serve the interests of the ruling class, and for the great majority of the people betray both love and beauty.

It was with the cultural revolution that Mao Tse-tung Thought really reached the entire Chinese people. And it was with this thinking that the people launched their attack on the political apparatuses which had begun to fossilize into institutions of privilege.

Now *Quotations from Chairman Mao Tse-tung* is found in every home in China. In most homes out in the countryside it is the first book the house has ever owned. Everyone is reading it or having it read aloud. It is no formal or ritualized reading, as of a catechism. In all discussions—How much manure? Where shall we invest? How solve the irrigation problem?—they start with Mao Tse-tung. In every question people are proceeding by discussion. No order, no decision from "above" is accepted without question. People are examining and discussing the contents of such decisions before implementing them. And in these discussions everyone has to take part and give his or her opinion.

What is holding China together is not an administrative apparatus. The apparatus has been cut down. And is still being cut down. It has a function, has its tasks to perform; but to decide China's destiny and be an abode of decision-makers is not one of them.

Nor is it the military that is holding China together. It exists. It is necessary. But it does not rule China. For several years now, the peasants at Liu Ling have had weapons in their homes.

What is holding China together is the discussion of Mao Tse-tung Thought. And that is why it is also correct to say that the fields are yielding better harvests because people's ways of thinking have been changed.

This means that each village, each brigade in the whole of China, is in a state of transformation. Everywhere new methods are being tried out. New methods for the school, new ways in production, new ways in income distribution. One brigade is not like another—even if both are based on the living study and application of Mao Tse-tung Thought. And this has meant the liberation of the Chinese people's power of initiative. The decisions do not come from Peking, as the decisions of decision-makers. They come in the form of general recommendations. Then, here and there, experiments are made, experiences spread, people learn from one another.

"Human nature" is being changed. All the hundreds of millions of Chinese are on the move, consciously discussing the future of their country, themselves making decisions, keeping a watchful eye on their leaders, shaping their own development through ceaseless general criticism and discussion. From all this a stupendous force is emerging.

There is nothing definitive about the cultural revolution. It has not created a "stable society." It is not a closed chapter:

> In the past we waged struggles in rural areas, in factories, in the cultural field, and we carried out the socialist education movement. But all this failed to solve the problem because we did not find a form, a method, to arouse the broad masses to expose our dark aspect openly, in an all-round way and from below. (Now we have found this form: it is the Great Proletarian Cultural Revolution—Lin Piao.)
>
> —Mao Tse-tung quoted in Lin Piao's *Report to the Ninth National Congress of the Communist Party of China*, April 1969

The present great cultural revolution is only the first; there will inevitably be many more in the future. The issue of who will win in the revolution can only be settled over a long historical period. If things are not properly handled, it is possible for a capitalist restoration to take place at any time. Let no one in the Party or among the people in our country think that everything will be all right after one or two cultural revolutions, or three or four. We must be very much on the alert and never lose vigilance.

> —Mao Tse-tung quoted in *Renmin Ribao*, May 23, 1967

We have won great victory. But the defeated class will still struggle. These people are still around and this class still exists. Therefore, we cannot speak of final victory. Not even for decades. We must not lose our vigilance. According to the Leninist viewpoint, the final victory of a socialist country not only requires the efforts of the proletariat and the broad masses of the people at home, but also involves the victory of the world revolution and the abolition of the system of exploitation of man by man over the whole globe, upon which all mankind will be emancipated. Therefore it is wrong to speak lightly of the final victory of the revolution in our country; it runs counter to Leninism and does not conform to facts.

— Mao Tse-tung quoted by Lin Piao in the *Report to the Ninth National Congress of the Communist Party of China,* April 1969

Thus when Liu Teh-ching, one cold dark evening in late autumn, stands in a schoolyard among the loess hills of Shensi, saying she has just come back from Peking and has seen Chairman Mao, and everyone cheers: This is not an expression of the people's humility towards a "great man." It is not Mao Tse-tung as an individual who is being cheered. The people are taking a political stand. They take a stand for Mao Tse-tung Thought.

Final Comment

It is not possible to understand what is happening in China today without having read Mao Tse-tung. I would suggest that you start with:

Quotations from Chairman Mao Tse-tung

and

Chairman Mao on continuing the revolution under the dictatorship of the proletariat.

It is preferable to read Mao Tse-tung in the editions he himself has authorized. This has to be pointed out because many "China-experts" are now at work, each one constructing his own "Mao Tse-tung." Talking about "authentic texts." Seemingly forgetting that Mao Tse-tung is a living writer. If you want to get a clear picture of the political thought of Stuart R. Schram, then of course you ought to read *The Political Thought of Mao Tse-tung* by Stuart R. Schram. If you are more interested in the political thought of Mao Tse-tung and find him more important than Schram, then of course you read Mao Tse-tung. His works are available. In editions he has published himself.

Lin Piao, *Report to the Ninth National Congress of the Communist Party of China* is an important document. Read it.

A Note on Transcription

The sinologically inclined reader will by now have seen that certain names are transcribed in a way that does not accord with any customary system of transcription of Chinese characters.

There is a very simple reason for this. In the autumn of 1962 I made a couple of errors in the transcription. Partly this was due to Pei Kwang-li making an erroneous transcription. But that was not her business to check, it was mine.

In December, 1962, I did correct the transcription. But then I had already written several long reports on Liu Ling for *VI,* the Swedish consumer cooperative magazine read by every fifth Swede. I found it important that the readers of that magazine would also be able to read the book. Thus I did not change the names in the book.

As I had not changed them then, I could not change them now. It is more important that the readers can check up on what was said by whom in 1962 and then in 1969, than that the transcription of some names are not in accordance with any generally used transcription system. (I toyed with the idea of using the Chinese transcription system. After all it is their language. But the reader would have difficulty in identifying Cao Zhen-qui with Tsao Chen-kuei.)

I most strongly advise the reader to read *Report from a Chinese Village.* Not because I have written it. But because it has been written. It gives the background, it makes it possible to compare what people are saying today with what they were saying in 1962.

A Note on the People in this Book

199

200

VINTAGE WORKS OF SCIENCE AND PSYCHOLOGY